Implementing Organizational Change

*A Practical Guide
to Managing
Change Efforts*

Gordon L. Lippitt
Petter Langseth
Jack Mossop

Implementing Organizational Change

 Jossey-Bass Publishers
San Francisco • Washington • London • 1985

82511

IMPLEMENTING ORGANIZATIONAL CHANGE
A Practical Guide to Managing Change Efforts
by Gordon L. Lippitt, Petter Langseth, Jack Mossop

Copyright © 1985 by: Jossey-Bass Inc., Publishers
433 California Street
San Francisco, California 94104

&

Jossey-Bass Limited
28 Banner Street
London EC1Y 8QE

Library of Congress Cataloging in Publication Data

Lippitt, Gordon L.
Implementing organizational change.

(A joint publication in the Jossey-Bass management
series and the Jossey-Bass social and behavioral science
series)
Bibliography: p. 173
Includes index.
1. Organizational change. 2. Management.
I. Langseth, Petter (date). II. Mossop, Jack (date).
III. Title. IV. Series: Jossey-Bass management series.
V. Series: Jossey-Bass social and behavioral science series.
HD58.8.L57   1985   658.4′063   84-47990
ISBN 0-87589-622-7 (alk. paper)

Manufactured in the United States of America

The paper in this book meets the guidelines for
permanence and durability of the Committee on
Production Guidelines for Book Longevity of the
Council on Library Resources.

JACKET DESIGN BY WILLI BAUM

FIRST EDITION

Code 8504

A joint publication in
The Jossey-Bass Management Series
and
The Jossey-Bass
Social and Behavioral Science Series

Consulting Editors
Human Resources

Leonard Nadler
Zeace Nadler
College Park, Maryland

This book is dedicated to our wives
Phyllis E. Lippitt, Sidsel H. Langseth,
and Mary Theresa Mossop

Preface

In this book we are reporting and sharing both concepts and practices applicable to organizational change that will increase systemwide effectiveness. Finding ways to accomplish such a goal is made urgent by the concern of managers who are wondering whether in a changing society they and their institutions can meet the demands for increased and improved delivery of products and services. In this vein, we think line managers will find herein some guidelines for ways to initiate a change process within their organization; staff specialists will discover the roles a support function can provide; organization development practitioners will see the functions of the process at work; consultants will be able to recognize the values inherent in using internal and external resources; those interested in evaluation will discover methods of measuring the effects of change; and managers, professors, students, and specialists can share with us an important case study of how large organizations may strive for excellence through participative management.

When we examine the trends affecting organization cultures, values, purposes, structure, process, and management, it is necessary to analyze the forces that affect such changes. Some of the more important of these are the greatly increased expectations worldwide for more services and a high standard of living; a widening gap between the powerful rich and the powerless poor; continued modifications in value systems; the intensified overreach of governments; the growing desire for influence on the part of minority groups; the burgeoning impact of mass media; the extensive development of and requirement for education; the shift from production economy to service economy; the knowledge and technology explosion; more and more activism by consumers and citizens; the evolution toward new avocations and vocations in society; more evident international interdependence; the passions of ecological concerns; the prevalent mobility of people that produces a lessened commitment to organization or community; the swelling size of social systems that tends to result in concepts of helplessness on the part of individuals; and, lastly, the greater desire for quality, not just quantity, as a goal in life.

These trends are accelerating at an uneven rate but at a speed that is challenging to all our institutions, as well as to the individuals who work within them. The overall picture aptly has been described as a transition from an industrial society to a postindustrial society, and it is readily realized that the inescapable changes are massive and out of control. We are all coping with this fundamental transition more slowly than it is occurring. Organization managers, particularly, in most instances are still managing with values, functional structure, and leadership styles that characterized the now dying industrial era.

The field of organization development has tended to focus on six major fields of activity: (1) individual skills training, both on and off the job, (2) interpersonal skills training, including T-group training, (3) management effectiveness training, including team building and fundamentals of managing, (4) intergroup change, including confrontation management and matrix management,

(5) total systems change, including restructuring communications and changing the management process, and (6) environment change, including open systems planning. These six basic changes are sometimes attempted by popular approaches that, as used, are all too often no more than unsubstantial, Band-Aid faddism. We include among these approaches quality circles, quality of work life, strategic planning, management by objectives, workers on the board, transactional analysis, autonomous work groups, operations research, and sensitivity training—when these approaches are taken out of the context in which they may succeed or when used in ignorance, desperation, or sheer mimicry. Faddism under these circumstances is at best an impetus for change in which the need to change is defined in terms of solutions available to an internal or external consultant or in terms of a supposed solution known to the client.

It is no longer sufficient to depend on remedial splinting of institutional fractures caused by excessive rigidity. Whether management is seen as a performing art or a profession, it mainly deals with the process of change—individual, group, or organizational. In less than twenty years, we have leapt from conventional to nuclear power, from piston age to jet age, from earth travel to space travel. Large and rapid changes are recurrent in our era, and they bring with them problems and challenges for those who manage people. Thus, coping with change primarily involves an understanding and utilization of human resources.

In this light, therefore, we believe our presentation will help our readers find answers to such questions as (1) How can we recognize changes that take place in the work environment? (2) Why is *change* such a frightening word to so many people? (3) What can we do about resistance to change? (4) Why do people not help with a needed change, rather than fight it every inch of the way? (5) How can change be effected with less frustration and difficulty?

Managers no longer can shrug knowledgeably and say, "You cannot change people." Research shows that people can change and be changed. In fact, people like change. What they resist are the *methods* managers use to cope with unexpected events or to put new ideas into effect. Here we have the two basic categories of change. One type is "unplanned," and it happens in and to all organizations: a tornado blows down a warehouse, a sharply higher interest rate comes along on bank loans, a principal officer dies. The other is "planned" and invokes the processes of organization development and renewal: a conscious, deliberate, and collaborative action to change a self-system, social system, or cultural system. Changes, planned or unplanned, are ubiquitous aspects of modern management. Unplanned changes can occur because of maturation, depressions, accidents, death, loss of resources, or external influences. Planned changes take place, among other reasons, because of the need for improved technology, new organizational structure, innovations for improving morale or productivity, or desirable new procedures.

If organization effectiveness through planned change is to become a reality, organization leaders must confront their present stage of functioning. We have found it essential that the manager examine with others the potential and future of his or her organization and establish for a five-year period ahead the goals and expectations for planning and action. In addition, implementing organizational change requires the development of skills on the part of those on the *inside* that will permit them to confront situations rather than await external confrontation by others who may have little real concern. Some of the elements to be confronted are determining the organization's true potential, developing open communications, enhancing human resources, and utilizing a systems approach to management in transition.

The choice available to managers today is between planning change in advance and stonewalling until change is forced by events. Planned change has an obvious advantage: It permits passing beyond reaction to anticipation, thus allowing management to influence directly the course of change. Coping with change through creative leadership makes it possible for an organization to become or remain viable, to adapt to new conditions, to solve problems, to learn from experience, and to move toward maturity. It also makes it possible to tolerate change, understand change, resist change when appropriate, and initiate change when needed.

This book is about planned change—and, in particular, about a two-year major change effort in the Administrative Department of the World Bank. We were involved in an attempt to strengthen the services, morale, and productivity of the department; thus, the change effort was given the name ADM Strengthening Project. Jack Mossop developed the project and was loaned to the project by the Personnel Department; Petter Langseth came to us from the Organization Planning Department; and Gordon Lippitt was a part-time consultant from George Washington University. This was one of the most thorough subsystem change efforts we know about in the field of organization development. Our experience with employee involvement, task forces, process observers, management support, and other aspects seems well worth sharing with others.

In our approach to planned change, we chose and continue to choose an eclectic path rather than limit our thinking to one best way from a single school of thought. We may borrow from each school of thought contingent on the client problem in hand. We try not to become hidebound to an approach that has worked well for us before but that may be inappropriate to the current problem. We attempt, by working together as a consultant team, to complement and broaden our mutual experience. However, our knowledge, skills, values, and experiences create a boundary around us that we try to break through and extend by also working with different colleagues so that we might grow. Our system is not perfect, but we approach each new client's problems so as to be of real help—without preconceptions as to the method we might use and with a deliberate effort to be multidisciplinary, interdisciplinary, and eclectic.

Such an eclectic methodology may well be anathema to those who prefer what they consider to be the one best way, the most favored school, or who wish always to follow their noses down the paths their experiences have laid out for them. In justice to them, it must be said that undoubtedly there are occasions when a simplistic way is best, when a particular pristine school of thought is most applicable. But, more often, a melding of applications is needed and more productive. It is increasingly difficult to draw from the past any one correct means of addressing and securing change in an organization. We have found that complex change circumstances demand the use of interdisciplinary teams of people

drafted from within and without the organization—people who can
borrow from a range of disciplines, failures, successes, and experiences rather than follow with excessive caution a thoroughly prescribed remedial procedure. At the World Bank, faithful to this
eclectic philosophy, we applied contingently eight distinct schools
of thought through the interventions of such interdisciplinary
teams.

The organization of this book is designed to be results
oriented. Although research *theory* is discussed in each chapter, we
also want to tell you about the practical reality of effecting changes
at the World Bank. Chapter One deals with ways to determine the
justification and need for change and explores three categories of
diagnosis that can help management plan the most desirable shape
and scope of improvement. It is clear that organization effectiveness
will mean different things to different organizations, and we offer
an eclectic approach that can be applicable to most situations. Ways
to develop unique criteria are discussed, and the example of the
World Bank project is presented.

In Chapter Two, we look at the planning for and initiating
of change and show how normal inertia can be overcome by going
beyond intentions to actions. Stages in planned change and ways to
secure involvement at each stage are demonstrated, and actual
application of these steps in a real case situation is explained.

The process of involving people in the change process,
including the training necessary to acquire the applicable skills, is
examined in Chapter Three. We explore the role of the task force
chairperson, facilitator, reporter/recorder, observer, and resource
person and also stress the need for deadlines and appropriate
procedures for setting and achieving targets.

Chapter Four spotlights practical ways to use task force and
process observers. We describe how to manage and lead task forces,
develop effective membership in these groups, and secure effective
group action. The importance of proper attention to systems at this
point in the change process is discussed, as well as support from
management for the task force work and recommendations.

Chapter Five examines the accountability process that ensures action. Change must be measured effectively through two-way
communications, clear objectives, measurable results, appropriate
involvement, a trusting climate, and supportive management. Implementation is the key to planning and without it effort and time

are wasted. Early success is the primary result of effective implementation.

In Chapter Six, the reader will find an explanation and examples of evaluation and methods of assessing change efforts. A model for looking at the evaluation process is given, with multiple methods for data collection. We also provide a report on the evaluation of the World Bank change project.

Learnings about organizational change efforts, with guidelines for practitioners, are presented in Chapter Seven. The difficulty in implementing change is acknowledged; however, we emphasize our belief that change can succeed if effective management values and practices are applied.

In preparing the manuscript for this book, we wish especially to express our appreciation to two officers of the World Bank: Martin J.W.M. Paijmans, vice-president for personnel and administration, for his early recognition of the need for implementing the ADM Strengthening Project; the project manager, William Cosgrove, director of administrative services, not only for the time and leadership he expended but also for his reading of the manuscript and his subsequent advice and counsel.

In conceptualizing the ADM Strengthening Project and in developing a case study approach, we were materially assisted by Robert Miles and Vijay Sathe of the Harvard Business School. We want to thank the Management Support Group, several of whom served as process observers—particularly Sam Niedzviecki, Rick Barry, Cliff Senf, and Jane Gouveia of the Coverdale Organization in Washington, D.C. We owe a debt of gratitude to the hardworking members of the ten task forces and the more than forty subtask forces that were essential to the success of the project. In the evaluation phase, we must recognize the fine administrative services of Mickey Yolles. And there is due a sense of obligation for the especially helpful guidance and textual suggestions contributed by Leonard and Zeace Nadler to the first draft of the manuscript. Lastly, but importantly, we are indebted to Reuben and Edith Stivers of Major Manuscripts for their final editing and typing.

Washington, D.C.   Gordon L. Lippitt
October, 1984   Petter Langseth
                                                              Jack Mossop

Contents

The Authors

Gordon L. Lippitt is professor of behavioral science in the School of Government and Business Administration at George Washington University. He is a charter member of the International Association of Applied Social Scientists, Inc., and a diplomate of the American Board of Professional Psychology. He received his B.S. degree in psychology from Springfield College (1942); his B.D. degree in psychology of religion from Yale University (1945); his M.A. degree in educational psychology from the University of Nebraska (1949); and his Ph.D. degree in social psychology from American University (1959).

Lippitt serves as president of Project Associates, Inc., and of the International Consultants Foundation; he also serves as chairman of the board for Organization Renewal, Inc., the International Institute for the Study of Systems Renewal, and Glenwood Manor

Farms, Inc. He has published more than three hundred articles, pamphlets, and books in the fields of human behavior, leadership, and organization effectiveness. His literary efforts include being coeditor of the *International Journal of Human Resource Development* (1980–81); guest columnist for *Nation's Cities Magazine* (1967–68); coeditor of *Optimizing Human Resources* (1971), *Management Development and Training Handbook* (1975), *Helping Across Cultures* (1979), and *Systems Thinking* (1981); coauthor of *Consulting Process in Action* (1978); and author of *Visualizing Change* (1973) and *Organization Renewal* (rev. ed., 1982).

Petter Langseth is a management consultant at the World Bank, coming to that position after serving in a similar role at the Norwegian Institute for Personnel Management in Oslo. His prior experience includes being assistant professor at the Oslo Business School and general management and personnel consultant in Europe, primarily at the Christiania Bank and Kreditkasse. He earned both M.A. (1973) and Ph.D. (1979) degrees in human resources management from the University of St. Gallen in Switzerland. Langseth's publications in Norwegian are *Active Personnel Work Today and Tomorrow* (3rd ed., 1978) and *How to Improve the Working Environment* (1980); and in German, *The Use of Autonomous Working Groups as a Tool to Increase Staff Participation in a Norwegian Bank* (doctoral thesis, 1979).

Jack Mossop is a personnel manager at the World Bank. He earned his M.A. degree (1977) in manpower studies from the Department of Occupational Psychology, Birkbeck College, University of London, and has completed additional postgraduate research at the Centre for Organization Studies at the University of Bath, England. Mossop has consulted in the field of human resource management in Europe and the United States for more than twenty years and has worked as an academic specialist in labor relations. Since 1971 he has been a fellow of the Institute of Personnel Management in England. His other primary professional interests are in the areas of organization development and innovative problem solving.

Implementing Organizational Change

*A Practical Guide
to Managing
Change Efforts*

Tomorrow a stranger will say with masterly good sense what we have thought and felt all the time, and we shall be forced to take with shame our own opinion from another.

Ralph Waldo Emerson

CHAPTER ONE

How to Diagnose an Organization's Need for Change

Before we delve into our efforts in the ADM (Administrative Services Department) Strengthening Project for the World Bank, it may be helpful to expose you to the overt manifestations of a need to change that overtake organizations from time to time and to how these demands can be brought to light for examination. In so doing, we will mention quite a few aspects of organization life, only some of which may apply directly to *your* organization. Necessarily throughout this book, we must trust to your good judgment when it comes to culling out those elements of need for change that are appropriate to commercial enterprise if your concern is with, say, change in an all-volunteer, nonprofit undertaking. In general, however, with a bit of psychological tolerance for exactitude of fit, almost everything about change is adaptable to almost every kind of organization.

Why Do We Need Organization Change?

The trends in society at large that affect human resources utilization tend to create a need for change. Lippitt (1983a) held interviews in the United States with chief executive officers of businesses, hospitals, government agencies, and nonprofit organizations in which he asked them their major concerns about human resources and from which he identified perceived needs generated by these concerns. Thirteen such common concerns were isolated:

Increased Organization Complexity. Executives say that change is needed more and more. *Prescription:* Develop the internal skills needed to enable change diagnosis within the organization.

Increased World Interdependence and Relationships. The United States is a multicultural country with multinational interests around the globe. Spanish, for example, will become a major language here in the next decade, affecting organizations at county and state levels. *Prescription:* Employ persons in the organization who are skilled in cross-cultural communications and relations.

Mission and Goal Coordination. Senior managers feel that they lack people who can set objectives, effectively coordinate getting things done, and achieve results. *Prescription:* Develop skills in producing goal clarity, goal coordination, and goal achievement.

Increased Interface Between Special Interest Groups, Government, Education, Business, and the Community. Managing an organization today involves interactions with and demands from regulatory bodies, interest groups in the community, and other businesses. Some top managers are bothered by the high quantity and low quality of meetings that this involves. *Prescription:* Make more effective use of communications skills, time/task management, and linking skills that can help connect organizations.

Maintaining Financial Perspectives. Executives are learning that their people too often lack sensitivity to financial matters. Constraints on spending and budget cutbacks are understood by too few. *Prescription:* Retain people who are skilled in financial realities and who can help others within the organization understand these verities.

New Organization Structures. New ways of organizing other than by hierarchy are occurring everywhere. Matrix processes, including multidisciplinary task forces, cut across functions and levels; form follows function, and the way of organizing follows the problem to be solved. *Prescription:* Employ people with skills in matrix management who can identify the skills needed and manage the temporary functional groups required to get problems solved.

Interunit Competition. With strident rivalries between departments, the focus moves away from solving problems to warfare between groups of people that are mutually dependent upon one another. *Prescription:* Make effective use of people skilled in collaboration.

Managing Change and Conflict. Senior managers spend one quarter of their time managing conflicts; hospital administrators spend 70 percent of their time in this way. *Prescription:* Have people at different levels in the organization who can manage and resolve conflict in a creative manner.

Changing Worker Values. People are questioning their work environment, their personal goals, their satisfaction with life. *Prescription:* Focus on the quality of working life in our organizations.

Clarifying Roles and Accountability. Too many people are unclear about their roles and their accountability within the organization. *Prescription:* Develop understanding of role negotiation and performance standards.

Effective Resource Utilization. Helping personnel grow and develop and giving them the right assignment is central to using resources effectively. Employees' lives do not end at the portals of their institutions; the growth fostered by the institution may be used in their outside lives as parents or volunteers. *Prescription:* Develop skills in human resources development, particularly coaching.

Increased Interface Between Machines and People. We need to learn more about the integration of human, financial, information, and mechanical systems. *Prescription:* Develop understanding of general system theory.

Finding Ways and Means to Increase Productivity. Good ideas die aborning because they originate in a perceived wrong place or with a supposedly wrong person. *Prescription:* Provide broad channels and ample opportunity for practical creativity to surface and to make itself known and appreciated.

Naisbitt (1982) analyzed for a ten-year period a large number of local, state, and nationwide newspapers in the United States and in the process identified ten social megatrends that affect some organizations by producing a need to change. He argues that these are bottom-up trends originating at the grass-roots level rather than top-down movements stimulated by institutions themselves. The trends involve movement: (1) from an industrial society to an information society; (2) from forced technology to high-tech/high-touch (face to face contact and communication between people); (3) from a national economy to a world economy; (4) from short-term to long-term concerns for the future; (5) from centralization to decentralization; (6) from institutional help to self-help; (7) from representative democracy to participative democracy; (8) from hierarchies to networking (people sharing ideas, information, and resources, thus creating linkages between people); (9) from North (decline of northern industry) to South (really West, Southwest, and Florida); and (10) from either/or (narrow choices) to multiple options.

Outside Impetus

A need to change can be and often is triggered from outside an organization. For example, the British Airports Authority, a nationalized industry, owns and operates Great Britain's major airports. It has faced a variety of changes from both within and without since its separation from the British Civil Service in 1966. Its civil service heritage, reinforced by its former civil service staff, made it difficult to build a profit-oriented organization that was relatively independent from government; all involved were decidedly unaccustomed to using profits, rather than government-appropriated money, to fund the capital development of the organization during the rapid growth in air transport over the last two decades. External pressures on the British Airports Authority has been extreme: The major trade unions involved at the airport fought a long battle against a new independent contractor offering airport services. The government pressured a relocation of headquarters from central London to Gatwick Airport and the establishment of a Scottish "divisional directorship." Community pressure groups opposed, repeatedly and effectively, both the proposed location of a third London airport and night flights into Heathrow Airport. The government's decision to join the European Economic

Community threatened profits from duty-free sales to its members. The development of the jumbo jet necessitated building new piers to accommodate both the aircraft and, more seriously, the 350 passengers disembarking and going through the airport—simultaneously with the arrival of another jumbo jet.

Another external influence that affects the need to change is the attitude of trade unions and employees. For example, in 1977, the London Borough of Harrow dealt with a strike in local government of up to 3,000 employees for a period of three weeks. This strike was called because the borough Authority abolished the vacant post of a cleaner at a public toilet and reduced by half the hours the toilet was open. Sometimes, the community pressures an organization. For instance, in 1969 the Ford Motor Company spent, at today's prices, over $20 million to install special equipment for filtering emissions from the Thames Foundry in Dagenham, near London—a response to sincere and valid community concern about health risks.

Beer (1980) believes that in the industrial setting both internal and external pressures establish a need for change. In the internal category he cites, among other causes, strikes; high levels of grievance, absenteeism, and turnover; threats of unionization; unacceptable numbers of factory rejects; wasted materials; insufficient quality of products; growing costs; and interdepartmental conflict. In the external category, to name a few, he includes price competition; new product rivalry; community dissatisfaction; consumer interest groups and complaints about quality and delivery; the interjection of governmental agencies; and adverse legislation. Tichy (1983), in contrast, credits need for change to a broader spectrum of causes, a shift in any one of which can set off a compeled adjustment. He uses the metaphor of a rope with political, cultural, and technical strands that appear as one and are interdependent—but that if separated and unraveled weaken the organization. Within this concept, Tichy says, organizations react with change whenever there is a modification of their environment, technology, goals, motivations, or perceived values. A number of authors also have pointed out that the need to change can be a response to the phases of an organization's life cycle—birth, youth, maturity—with each phase having distinct concerns and consequences. It can be seen, therefore, that forces for change exerted on organizations are many, varied, dynamic, and complex. They are the greatest and most constant challenge faced by management.

Three Major Categories of Diagnosis

Thompson (1967) argues that diagnosis is useful if it provides information—not on accomplishment or nonaccomplishment, but rather with respect to ability to take an action in the future. In this context, Tichy (1983) proposes three categories of diagnosis: (1) *Radar scan,* which involves quickly scanning an entire organization in order to identify "blips" or trouble spots; this method is superficial and requires a model but may provide an incentive to undertake directed in-depth analysis. (2) *Symptom focused,* which carries the danger of ending up treating symptoms rather than underlying causes but which enables the diagnostician to delve where trouble is known to exist. (3) *In-depth,* a systematic, detailed analysis of an organization; it requires the preparation of a model by which to be guided and with which to interrelate the data obtained.

A Framework for Diagnosing an Organization's Need for Change

A meaningful and useful diagnostic model has been a long time in development. The state of the art is such that today McCaskey's (1981) six-box diagram has been improved by the addition of a seventh box by Georgiades and Wilkinson (1983) in order to encompass the important elements of physical setting and technology. This latest diagnostic model is illustrated in Figure 1. The appropriate order of use is to start with the context in which an organization exists and thereafter to examine in sequence organization culture, task requirements, formal organization, people, and physical setting and technology. The seven boxes in Figure 1 are numbered in this order. A schedule of several questions related to each box was developed by Georgiades and Wilkinson (1983) for course materials and by Tichy (1983) for a book. We adapted these questions to the ADM Strengthening Project as follows:

**Figure 1. The Seven-Box Diagnostic Model
for Analyzing an Organization's Needs.**

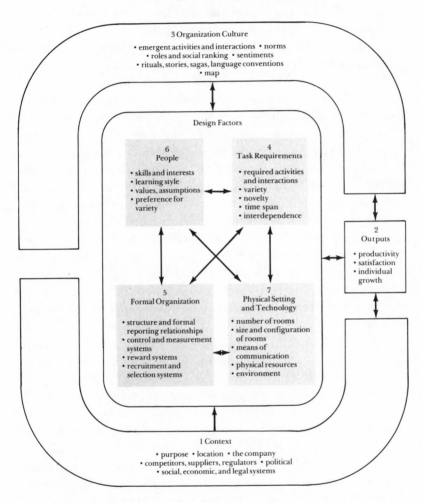

Source: From Michael B. McCaskey, *Framework for Analyzing Work Groups.* Case 9-480-009. Cambridge, Mass.: Harvard Business School Course Services, 1981, p. 21. Amended and used with permission.

1. **Context.** *Purpose:* What are the organization's beliefs? What are its products or services? Have these changed over time? Who are the principal stakeholders? What do they expect? What were the critical events in the history of the organization? What significant leadership changes have taken place? What is the history of the organization's profits? Have there been financial difficulties or large surpluses? What have been the significant technological changes? How have the sales and marketing concept and function changed? How has the market share changed? Have there been difficult employee relations issues? At what stage is the organization in its life cycle? What are the special problems being experienced at its life cycle stage? *Location:* How does the location of the organization affect its performance? How does the organization contribute to or detract from the well-being of the community? Are there environmental issues with which the organization is struggling? *Competitors:* Who are the organization's competitors? How has the competition changed? How has the organization weathered these changes in competition? *Suppliers:* What is the organization's experience with respect to suppliers' quality, delivery, and price? Is this getting better or worse? *Regulators:* How does federal or state legislation and regulation affect the organization? How is this changing? *Political, social, economic, and legal systems:* How have these systems affected the organization in the past and at present?

2. **Outputs.** *Organizational level:* What is the match within the organization between inputs and outputs in terms of profitability and productivity, efficiency, rate of return, number of objectives achieved, customer satisfaction, community well-being, employee relations, and the importance of output relative to the amount of input? *Group level:* Judging from indicators of morale and cohesiveness, do employees appear to want to stay with the organization? What is the absentee rate, what is the employee turnover rate, and what is the requested reassignment rate? Is there inappropriate conflict within or between groups? *Individual level:* What reading is obtained from general satisfaction indicators? Do personal adjustment indicators show that employees feel they have good future prospects? What is their level of self-esteem? Are employees committed to the organization's goals? Do employees exhibit growth, openness, trust, candor, and confidence, or do they appear to feel

threatened and vulnerable? Are there indications of undue stress, such as excessive sickness and accidents?

3. Organization Culture. *Identifying your culture:* Which of these generic cultures (see Deal and Kennedy, 1982) best describes the organization: tough guy (high risk, quick feedback); work hard/ play hard (fun, few risks, quick feedback); bet the company (high risk, slow feedback); or process (the *how* is more important than the *what*)? What description of the organization's culture do you obtain from studying the physical setting across sites, functions, and levels; from reading what your organization says about its own culture in annual reports and press releases; from how it greets strangers; from asking employees about myths, communications, why the company is successful, what explains its growth, what kind of people work there, who gets ahead in the long run, what kind of a place it is to work in, what an average day is like, and how things get done (rituals, meetings, bureaucratic procedures); from observing how people spend their time as compared to what they say they do; and from analyzing what is being discussed and written about the company? *Signs of a culture in trouble:* Which of these indicators does your organization demonstrate?: no value concepts about how to succeed, too many beliefs about how to succeed, different parts of the organization have fundamentally different beliefs, heroes are considered disruptive or destructive, rituals are disorganized or contradictory, organization has an inward and short-term focus and gives little emphasis to outputs, or clashes occur that disrupt the organization? *Norms:* What norms apply within the organization with respect to length of work day, participation in group meetings (who speaks most and to whom), dealing with interpersonal conflict, dealing with power and authority, and telling the truth (at different levels in the hierarchy and among peers)? How are decisions made? How are problems solved? Do employees feel that their part of the organization is a team or only a collection of individuals? Is feedback within the organization viewed as something to be avoided or encouraged, as supportive or damaging, as timely or delayed? *Emergent activities and interactions:* What patterns of behavior are inventions by individuals in response to the needs of their task and social context? Do these patterns of behavior affect the organization's performance for better or worse? *Rituals,* *stories, and language:* What do these manifestations tell you about the organization's culture? *Axioms:* What important rules about procedure and conduct has the organization adopted, such as "salesmen must press the flesh with customers"? How have these axioms facilitated or hindered organizational decisions and interaction with others?

4. Task Requirements. *Tasks:* What are the principal tasks members of the organization must perform, and how do these tasks interface with each other? Does each employee have an up-to-date job description? Do these job descriptions tend to restrict or confine the employees to whom they apply? Is each job description compatible with the employee's need to involve the use of different skills? Is there task significance in relation to the tasks performed by others? Is there task identity that requires doing a particular job from beginning to end? Is there personal autonomy that provides relative freedom, independence, and discretion in scheduling work and determining the procedures used, and is there job feedback concerning effectiveness of performance? Is such feedback being usefully disseminated and acted on? *Goals:* Are the organization's goals clearly defined? Are these goals understood and accepted by the organization's executives? Do employees know what is expected of them in terms of these goals? Are the accepted standards of performance related to these goals? *Roles:* How mutually interdependent are employees' tasks? Is such interdependence valued by the organization? *Procedures:* How clearly prescribed are the procedures for getting things done within the organization? Is the informal network of influence stronger than the formal, prescribed administrative procedures?

5. Formal Organization. *Differentiation:* How is work organized vertically and horizontally? How well does this succeed? How are authority, responsibility, and accountability allocated for outputs and resources? Is the organization's hierarchy adaptable to change? Why is each level needed? Does the formal structure facilitate or hinder communication and problem solving? What are the patterns of reporting relationships? Why are these patterns valid? Can the informal structure be clearly diagrammed? *Integration:* How is work coordinated in terms of policy, procedures, programs, hierarchy, planning, upward information systems, downward information systems, lateral information systems, liaison personnel, task forces, matrix structure, and foci of cost and profit? How well is the work of the organization coordinated? What is the reward system, and how highly is it respected by the employees of the organization? What are the recruitment and selection procedures? Is the organization recruiting people with the right skills and attitudes?

6. **People.** *Working-level employees:* How many employees does the organization have—by location, level, occupational group, and so forth? Do they possess the skills needed in their assignments within the organization? Are any employees overqualified for their assignments? What do employees say they like or dislike about their work? What do they say about their physical environment? To what extent do they feel their assignment has allowed them to improve and grow? How are employees trained inside the organization? *Managerial and supervisory employees:* In this context, what are the answers to each of the questions posed above with respect to employees? Is there an appropriate balance of technical and managerial employees? Are managers and supervisors the sole source of work integration within the organization? Assess the managerial skills in terms of planning, goal setting, budgeting, implementing decisions, evaluation, coaching, writing, presentations, decision making, small-group leadership, emotional support, and counseling. On the basis of this analysis, what is the management development track record? Do the managers of the organization have similar psychological profiles? *Top managers:* Do the organization's top managers tend to be figureheads? Do they set the tone for the organization, monitor what is going on, maintain liaison with all parts of the organization, disseminate information? Do they act as spokespersons for the organization, possess entrepreneurial attitudes, properly handle disruptive occurrences, allocate resources, successfully negotiate on behalf of the organization?

7. **Physical Setting and Technology.** What is the technological level achieved by the organization? How does this affect the employees, customers, and community? Is this technological level higher or lower than is appropriate to the needs of the organization? Are significant changes planned? Are employees trained to use the technology advantageously? Is the technological equipment well

maintained? Are rooms and space within the organization's prop-
erty designed and allocated on the basis of task need or on the basis
of status? How does the physical environment affect employees'
performance of assigned tasks? Does the physical environment
facilitate team behavior?

Other Practical Guidelines

In a way, the seven-box examination of needs, depending as
it does on subjective responses to more or less externally posed
queries, provides something more of a study of organization character and malaise than a critical probe of symptoms leading to
identification of physical and attitudinal disabilities. Nevertheless,
the seven-box approach unquestionably is an excellent preliminary
procedure. We found, however, that any one of three other means
of diagnostic inquiry would supply a more practical audit.

1. Open Systems Planning. A particularly down-to-earth
means of participative analysis is offered by Jayaram (1976). His
process begins, first, by appointing a person who is facile in the
skill of open systems planning, in which some prediagnosis would
be helpful, and, second, by gathering under this facilitator's direction for three days as many as is feasible of the influential and
informed members of the subject organization—certainly the board
of directors or one level lower, but not necessarily excluding the
known leaders of the informal influence network. What is essential
is that those so assembled have the power and legitimacy to obtain
answers to their own questions, the authority to make decisions,
and the group process skills and mutual trust required to labor
together effectively toward a common diagnostic goal. A general
abstract of this procedure is shown in Table 1.

2. Action Research. Here diagnosis is effected by collecting
data concerning four levels within the organization: the organization itself, the subdivisions into which it is functionally separated,
the managerial echelon, and the individuals who comprise the work
force at all levels. At each of the four levels, the spotlight of
inquiry—in a prescribed order of interview, observation, questionnaire, and performance measurement—is directed toward in-
vestigating such topics as satisfaction, effectiveness, efficiency,

Table 1. Open Systems Planning.

Activity: Creation of Present Scenario

Group Actions	Facilitator Actions
External Environment	

Group Actions	Facilitator Actions
• Concentrates on one system, such as a factory or hospital.	• Asks: "What is expected of this system?"
• Lists all expectations on selected system from external environment.	• Encourages sharing of individual perceptions of the outside world.
• Classifies expectations according to source (domains of expectation).	• Records or gets group to record ideas in pictures and words on newsprint sheets and attaches sheets to wall.
• Identifies domains left out and/or expectations for which there is no source traceable and/or obvious domains for which the expectations are not clear.	• May synthesize data or have group perform synthesis.
• Distinguishes among domains shared and unshared and contradictory expectations.	• Helps evoke high level of creativity, including the use of metaphors.
• May reprepare its first scenario with greater insight.	• Encourages participation.
	• Asks: "Who expects this?"

Internal Environment

Group Actions	Facilitator Actions
• Identifies and describes the system from its center to its peripheries in all its complexities and richness.	• Encourages group to look for intra- and interpersonal subsystemic expectations.
• Analyzes itself by activities, interactions, and sentiments.	• Narrows or broadens the band of search according to political climate, group cohesiveness, trust within group and between individuals.
	• Encourages creativity by asking: "What would you give up if you had to give up 90 percent of what you are as a system?
	• Asks where the tensions and energies are.

Value Systems

Group Actions	Facilitator Actions
• Traces and records value systems prevalent in each external domain.	• Asks: "Who expects whom to do what?"
• Repeats for internal environment.	• Records anecdotes, phrases.
	• Prepares for gloom and blame by group, "hangs in" and helps group to do the same.

Table 1. (Cont'd)

Activity: Creation of Realistic Future Scenarios

Group Actions	Facilitator Actions
• Defines a realistic future scenario. • Goes through the same steps as in the creation of the present scenario and projects the effects of its present value systems.	• Asks: "If the curve from past to present is projected to the future, where will the organization be three and five years from now?" • Notes suppressed feelings, positive or negative, about present trends.

Activity: Creation of Idealistic Future Scenarios

Group Actions	Facilitator Actions
• Answers the question: "What alternative futures would you like to create?" or "If you had the power to change anything in the previous scenarios, what would you change, and how would the scenario look when changed?"	• Asks the group to split into dyads or triads. • Encourages members of group to dream unfettered by realities. • Helps creativity to emerge.

Activity: Sharing of Idealistic Future Scenarios

Group/Individual Actions	Facilitator Actions
• Each small group presents to the whole group its idealistic future scenario. • Each individual asks himself and others: "If the suggested changes take place, how will other things be affected in terms of quality and quantity?" • Group asks: "What variances are there between (a) the present and idealistic futures and (b) the realistic and idealistic futures, and why?" • Group prepares three lists: yes, maybe, yes-no.	• Reminds group to perceive all relevant dimensions of the casual aspects of environment, such as political/legal, economic, and ecological, and the effect change might have on such aspects of the environment. • Decides whether to encourage or discourage greater complexity. • Presents all previous scenarios. • Speculates: "Can you do anything about absorbing the variances with enough lead time? If so, what? If not, why not?" • Records reasons given for each item appearing on the three lists and, if needed, asks for more information.

Table 1. (Cont'd)

Activity: Temporal Planning

Group Actions	Facilitator Actions
• Examines the three lists and asks: "What can be done about each item tomorrow, six months from now, two years from now?" • Decides on choice of interventions it will make. • Decides if open systems planning should be repeated at other levels in the organization. • Decides on a follow-up schedule by which to share the flow of action steps and update the scenarios.	• Helps group address such questions as: "Why intervene at all, what kind of intervention and why, where to intervene and why there, why proceed toward that future?" • Helps group with concrete action planning for the yes list. • Helps group find the causes of disagreements for the yes-no list, such as ideology, values, strategy operation, or tactics. • Helps group decide what additional data or participation is needed for resolution of the maybe list.

performance, stress, aspiration, and acceptance. As originated by Margulies and Wallace (1972), the data collected is treated as confidential, as are the derived assumptions concerning attitudes and perceptions.

Once in hand, the semi-raw data is categorized and fed back to carefully defined and designed work groups for evaluation and summarization. The product of this process is then recycled at each of the four levels through revised interviews, observation, and questionnaires. Though time consuming, this procedure has the merit of being an ongoing process that attempts to take into account the ongoing changes in the real world. As pointed out by Huse (1980), however, such an involved process demands the assistance and guidance of a professional behavioral scientist, if only to enable the leaders of the organization to understand the diagnoses as they are achieved.

3. Looking for Trouble. An eminently powerful and succinct model for organizational diagnosis has been presented by Weisbord (1978)—although it lacks strength in developing historical and cultural background. He calls it "six places to look for trouble": (1) *Leadership:* There must be someone who keeps the other five elements in balance. (2) *Purposes:* The persons concerned must understand what business they are in. (3) *Structure:* The workload must be divided appropriately. (4) *Helpful Mechanisms:* The best possible arrangements must be made for coordinating technologies. (5) *Relationships:* Both competing technologies and conflict among people must be ably managed. (6) *Rewards:* Is there an incentive for doing all that needs to be done?

Concurrently with the use of this model, Weisbord encourages the members of the various levels of the organization to give serious thought to three groups of penetrating inquiries:

1. Define the organization's boundaries. List three important environmental demands that influence the organization's strategic mission. List the important inputs, outputs, and sources of feedback. Describe the transformation process of inputs into outputs. Decide what the organization does that makes it unique.
2. Select one major output and trace its relationship to the whole system. Record "what is" and "what ought to be." In view of the foregoing, evaluate the level of satisfaction on the part of producers and customers. Explain what is right and what is wrong and how the selected output is thereby affected.
3. Consider whether the demands of customers, suppliers, competitors, regulatory groups, and the parent organization are causing a strain at one or more of the six possible trouble spots. Consider whether poor managerial or supervisory coping with internal issues is creating undue stress within important organizational domains. State what influence any particular individual has over the situation.

It is appropriate at this stage of our discussion of organization diagnosis to post something of a caution sign. The hard kernels of quintessential data, those that ring true, those so self-evident that no honest-hearted board member can deny their validity, simply are not all that easy to come by—regardless of methodologies of diagnosis earnestly applied. As with most revelations, the needed thought strikes from out of the blue when least expected—and then perhaps only when there exists a certain amount of open-minded receptiveness. Most of the time, the useful, meaningful essence of organization diagnosis is likely to be as elusive as the "dark pearl of Tao" in the parable so beautifully narrated by the twelfth-century philosopher, Chuang-tse. "On his way back from the Mountain, the Yellow Emperor lost the dark pearl of Tao. He sent Knowledge to find it, but Knowledge was unable to understand it. He sent Distant Vision, but Distant Vision was unable to see it. He sent Eloquence, but Eloquence was unable to describe it. Finally, the Emperor sent Empty Mind, and Empty Mind came back with the pearl" [Hoff, 1983, p. 143].

Data Collection During the Change Process

Frequently recognized problems are derived from a variety of sources during data collection. Ongoing data collection is essential during the change project in order to guide the process, to evaluate various events, to assemble data that identify needed actions, and to provide management with information about progress toward goals. One example of the use of such data occurred in a five-phase change project used in a large insurance company. The managers of this sizable (and profitable) company had recently initiated a coordinated program involving management by objectives and organization development in order to attack some of their concerns about channeling talent, ideas, and conflict toward institutional goals. The five phases were:

Identifying Common Denominators. During this process, individuals from all departments identified goals that they felt were important. From this input, a group consensus was formed with which most of the employees could identify. This provided a base and a common denominator with which people could reasonably, easily relate and interrelate.

Administering Organization Strengths and Human Resources Inventory. This phase helped identify resources that could be directed toward accomplishing predetermined goals. A set of forms was presented that helped reveal previously untapped capabilities and interests in the work force. This resulted in a better awareness of the total potential of the workers and assisted in the redistribution of responsibilities.

Establishing Objectives. Measurable departmental and individual objectives were determined, which made it possible to correlate resources with objectives. This also reinforced commitment through participation.

Measuring Results. What had been accomplished was gauged on the basis of group as well as individual performance. These standards of evaluation were developed and agreed upon by the participants. This enabled a "self-policing" concept to be introduced, which also improved individual motivation.

Reinforcing Good Results. Performance planning and employee appraisals emphasized the strengthening of good performance rather than the disciplining of poor behavior. This tended to build rather than destroy a person's self-image and increase his or her ability to contribute.

The long-term results of the program have yet to be measured. There are, however, some good indications. The results so far support the theories that: (1) People tend to support what they participate in. (2) Most people want to do a good job (given the opportunity and assistance they need). (3) People need encouragement more than they need criticism. (4) Management by objectives and organization development projects tend to support one another. (5) Real participation is a strong motivator. (6) Building on strengths is better than focusing on weaknesses.

In another example (see discussion of the World Bank later in this chapter), the task forces in the World Bank's ADM Strengthening Project used employee data collected early in the process to identify those issues, concerns, and problems that needed approval by top management and/or action by the work groups. An employee survey also took place at the World Bank during the ADM Strengthening Project that was fed into the process of change. Such data, however it is collected, may be used to provide feedback to participants, to identify areas for skill training, to give early warning of the need for conflict resolution (particularly that arising from the consequences of change in progress), and to examine events and accomplishments at predetermined milestones in the change process. Regularly assessing the effect and contribution of each of these types of events throughout the change process can provide important information useful in designing future projects, improving similar events scheduled to take place in the current project, and guiding the preparation of the next process of data collection.

The collection of data *during* the change process, by whatever mode or means of audit, should have as its primary purpose the guidance and control of the process itself. It thus enables management to: (1) *Identify strengths in the change process.* Employees generally affirm more strong points than weak points; it is encouraging for any organization to have its idea of what is "going right" reinforced. (2) *Pinpoint problem areas in the change process.* Detailed analysis of data screens isolated complaints and directs attention to those areas that need specific and significant improvement. (3) *Encourage more open communication as a part of the change process.* As employees become aware that management is open to feedback, direct lines of communication are brought into being. (4) *Plan for necessary modifications in the change process.* It provides specific options for action with respect to identified problem areas. (5) *Provide stimulus for introducing alterations in the change process.* It creates a motivation to seek out ways to carry out recommended improvements in productivity, quality, and working conditions.

The World Bank

The overriding purpose of the World Bank is to promote economic and social progress in developing nations by helping them raise their productivity and thus their standard of living. Thus, the World Bank has three principal functions: to lend money, to provide advice, and to facilitate investment by others.

The bank is comprised of three institutions: The International Bank for Reconstruction and Development, the International Development Association, and the International Finance Corporation. Its headquarters and 95 percent of its employees, many of whom travel extensively throughout the world on the business of the bank, are located in Washington, D.C.

The International Bank for Reconstruction and Development (IBRD), oldest of the three institutions, was established in 1945 by representatives of 44 nations that were concerned about postwar reconstruction and decolonization and the financial resources they would require. Today, the IBRD is owned by more than 140 countries. Since its beginning, it has lent in excess of $105 billion for more than 3,000 projects in over 100 countries, primarily to meet the foreign exchange costs of development projects and to ensure the developing nations full value by requiring international competitive bidding for goods and services procured with bank funds. Loans are made to creditworthy borrowers, but only for projects that promise a high rate of economic return. In this sense, therefore, the IBRD is both a lending institution and a development agency. Most of its funds are obtained through medium- and long-term borrowing in the world's capital markets at no cost to its member nations. The IBRD earned a net income of about $600 million in each of the fiscal years 1981 and 1982.

The International Development Association (IDA) has the same objectives, policies, standards, and staff as the IBRD. Its distinction is that it lends to the poorest countries, which could not obtain IBRD or other financing at regular market rates and terms because they are not considered creditworthy. The IDA charges only commitment and service fees of less than 1 percent on its credits, which have fifty-year amortization with a ten-year grace period. The IDA was established in 1960 and has lent nearly $30 billion for over 1,300 projects since its inception. The primary source of the IDA's funds is contributions provided mainly by the richer countries.

The International Finance Corporation (IFC) both lends to and takes equity positions in private-sector companies without government guarantees. The IFC was established in 1956 and has a separate operational staff from IBRD/IDA. Its function is to assist the economic development of less-developed countries by promoting growth in the private sector of their economies and helping mobilize domestic and foreign capital for this purpose. The IFC has invested around $5 billion in over 700 ventures.

The Administrative Services Department of the World Bank Group has ten divisions that provide sixty-nine different services for headquarters personnel. These services include building maintenance, cartography, communications, cleaning, graphics, interpretation, office supplies, printing, purchasing, records management, restaurants, shipping, translation, and travel. The department has 530 full-time employees and, in addition, uses the services of 1,200 full- and part-time contract personnel.

Our Eclectic Approach to Organizational Change

At the World Bank, the ADM Strengthening Project was initiated by concern over informally assembled data that indicated a frequency of complaints from client departments in the bank, some swampy areas of low morale and lessened productivity, and voiced and unvoiced dissatisfaction with the bank's performance as a contractor. Top management realized an urge to action. But, as consultants to this effort, we were aware that both scholars and practitioners have been unable to agree on the meaning and measurement of organization effectiveness. In the literature, some authors define the effectiveness of an organization in terms of ability to reach goals; others talk in terms of ability to acquire scarce and valued resources. Some consultants write about an organization's capacity to satisfy its members, others about the facility with which productivity is combined with flexibility. Such confusion is more than semantic. Organizations are complex, and adequate models of organization functioning are in short supply.

As Campbell states (Miles, 1980, p. 359): "Effectiveness is not *one* thing. An organization can be effective or ineffective on a number of different facets that may be relatively independent of one another. . . . Perhaps a better way to think of organizational effectiveness is as an underlying construct that has no necessary and sufficient *operational* definition but that constitutes a model of theory of what organizational effectiveness is."

In light of this confusion, it seems worthwhile to examine the various "schools of thought" applicable to organization effectiveness. One colleague (Miles, 1980) has identified eight such schools into which the advocacies of writers, researchers, scholars, practitioners, and organizational change specialists/consultants align themselves:

School of Thought	*Effectiveness Focus*
Scientific management school	Control and efficiency
Human relations school	Interface between individual and organization
Sociotechnical school	Optimization of both technical and social systems
Organization development school	Interpersonal and intergroup linkages with openness of communication and teamwork
Microeconomics school	Profit and return on investment
Goal attainment school	Productivity, results, or ultimate goals
Systems model school	Interdependencies of multiple factors and functions
Integrated model school	Satisfaction of multiple constituencies in a continuous process of strategic renewal

In our eclectic approach at the World Bank, of course, we by definition avoided adopting in its entirety any one of these advocacies. The first step in our approach to diagnosis was to obtain recommendations for change within the department from managerial and nonmanagerial employees who were experts in the diverse and complex services provided. The second step involved our participation in a two-week training seminar at the Harvard Business School, which dealt with a range of case studies on organizational change. During the seminar, we completed a preliminary diagnosis—using the framework shown in Figure 1—of the needs for change in the Administrative Services Department. A third step toward diagnosis was that of establishing a support group of World Bank specialists possessing a wide span of expertise in administration and management. This group acted as a foil against which to test the preliminary diagnosis derived at the Harvard Business School. Lastly, ten task forces, one for each division of the department, were charged with undertaking a detailed examination of change needs. The knowledge, time, and skills available within each task force were supplemented by the expertise of the consultants and members of the support group; and, where desirable, specific training was given. The support group analyzed the diagnoses and recommendations of each task force and, as much as was considered advisable, recommended modifications. These modifications were reconsidered by the respective task forces; in this manner, an ultimate refinement was achieved by passing the recommendations up and down the administrative chain of authority for open-minded discussion and evaluation. Against this procedural background, we eclectically selected and implemented six basic approaches to effectiveness:

Planned and Coordinated Change Activities. Realizing that in a change effort involving appropriate people participation tends to become a complex project, we felt a need for a detailed plan and well-managed coordination. As a result, the major phases of this change effort were planned and discussed with those concerned at the upper levels, which resulted in the establishment of several coordination mechanisms, such as a support group, a project management team, scheduled goals, and professional process consultation. Thus, we borrowed from the scientific management school and from the goal attainment school.

Participative Management Advocacy. It was determined that the ADM Strengthening Project should demonstrate on the part of management a participative philosophy, even though such a management style was not typical of the department. The feeling was that all employees in the Administrative Services Department should be involved in identifying needs and concerns, as well as in electing their own task forces to work on the issues raised in their own divisions. In addition, internal specialist resources were utilized in order to create a minimal need for outside consultants. The department's front office management personnel also committed themselves to change and organized their own task force. This participative approach was our attempt to integrate into our work the important findings of the human relations school, the organization development school, and the integrated model school. We chose to do this because the diversity and complexity of most of the administrative services demanded input from hundreds of people in the organization.

Action Research Effort. This approach was used in the change process, and managerial and nonmanagerial employees were enlisted as data collectors, data providers, and action takers. Such an approach was reinforced by the internal structure, guidance, review procedures, and follow-up functions provided by the support group; this action research mode was further supported by providing for each task force—especially the chairman—training in the involvement process that ensured a higher level of competence. Borrowed from the organization development school, requiring as it does continual evaluation and replanning, this action research approach enabled the World Bank to fulfill its desire to learn by doing.

Accountability Focus. The change process is best managed through delegation of accountabilities. This implies not only that there are means to guide and control the process but also that each part of the process and its outcomes is the explicit responsibility of some particular person. At the World Bank, such responsibilities were delegated from the department director, through the project management team, down to the chairman of each task force. Milestones for delivery of certain products and services were agreed upon and monitored. The focus of responsibility and the results of the process are borrowed from the goal attainment school and the microeconomics school.

Results-Oriented Implementation. Each of the ten task forces agreed to a timetable for completion of each phase of the change effort (see Table 2) and for presenting its work to the support group for comment and approval. The division line managers were held responsible for implementing each task force's action plan. In many cases, the task forces suggested the names of people who would implement a part of a plan. Getting things done was emphasized throughout this project, and this was a vital mind-set for the managers in planning the diagnosis and implementing the changes. This approach owes its origins to the goal attainment school.

Open Sociotechnical Systems. The sociotechnical approach advocates a close relationship between the structure and the objectives of an organization and between the organization's working environment and the technologies applied by the organization.

These relationships were important at the World Bank because improvements in technical efficiency and working environment were both to be highlighted with equal emphasis. The open systems thinking was activated by analyzing the interface between the World Bank as a system and its Administrative Services Department as a subsystem—and then examining the Administrative Services Department as a system and its ten divisions as subsystems. All of this leaned heavily on the sociotechnical school and the systems model school.

Table 2. Key Milestones in the ADM Strengthening Project.

Milestones	Date
Preconditioning	
Organization planning department study	July 1981
Kick-off meeting	October 1981
Setting Up Structure	
Appoint support group, process consultant, and project management	February 1982
Elect task forces	March 1982
Data Collection	
Questionnaire to all staff	March 1982
Training of task forces	May 1982
Analysis of Data	
Ten task forces and forty sub-task forces analyze data	June–October 1982
Recommendations	
Deadline for submission of action plans	December 1982
Immediate Reaction Evaluation	May 1982
Implementation	
Deadline for implementation of action plans	December 1983
Second stage of evaluation	June 1984
Follow-Up	
Communicate follow-up action to all staff	April 1984
Objective setting for FY85 to be completed	July 1984

Reflective Comments

In diagnosing the Administrative Department's need for
change, we reaffirmed the virtue of an eclectic approach that
borrows from an array of theories and empirical experiences—
eliminating the mumbo-jumbo so as to achieve practical and simple
concepts applicable to *this* change effort. We also learned how true
it is that people who possess the power to affect the organization's
future must take leading roles in undertaking the diagnosis—and
this simply must include managerial and nonmanagerial employees
at *all* levels of the organization; a primary concern that developed
during the diagnosis was that some of the data to be collected, and
some of the recommendations apparently to be made, would involve
policies and practices that are not under the control of the department engaging in the change process.

CHAPTER TWO

How to Initiate and Plan the Change Process

Organizational change efforts, whether classified as systems development, organization renewal, problem-solving processes, strengthening programs, or organization development, all have one thing in common: They all are processes initiated in order to achieve some organization objective and to solve problems. In German management science literature, the term *systems development* often is used as a translation for *organization development*. The systems development school of thought is based more on cybernetics than on the traditional organization development school in the United States, which is based more on behavioral science.

Organization Development as a Planned, Systematic Problem-Solving Process

According to Rush (1974, p. 32), an organization development process is "a planned, managed, systematic process to change the culture, systems and behavior of an organization, in order to improve the organization's effectiveness in solving its problems and achieving its objectives." Stated more simplistically, organization development is a group of activities initiated in order to enhance the organization's productivity and the job satisfaction of its personnel. Depending on the values in the organization, more or less emphasis is put on productivity and the working environment.

The organization development process is issue oriented, focusing on existing and anticipated organization problems. In most cases, a problem-solving process will focus on identification and description of problems, neutralization of the forces that create the problems, recommendations on how to solve the problem, with pros and cons to each alternative, decisions among alternatives, implementation of action plans, and evaluation of what has or has not been achieved.

The mere fact that objectives of some kind exist implies that thought and planning have gone into deciding where the organization wants to go, and the problem-centered nature of organization development implies that the organization can identify and cope with restraining forces, whether they are externally or internally generated. Thus, organization development is prescriptive in that it calls for change in a desired direction. The elements of the prescription are interrelated and mutually reinforcing, as indicated by a reexamination of the definition of organization development, its implications, and its underlying values.

In order to describe organization development in more detail, we can use a broader definition adapted from Rush (1974):

• Organization development is, most importantly, *a process*. Any process shows continuous change over time, as contrasted with a static or time-bound effort. Process connotes a series of interacting functions aimed at a logical goal.

• *Change* lies at the heart of organization development, and it has as its target the elements of growth, effectiveness, and excellence, thus implying that the organization is an open system that is capable of improvement on individual, group, and organization levels.

• *Planned change* involves a series of reinforcing activities undertaken with purpose and intent rather than something that happens accidentally. Planned change further invokes a decision about the direction a process should take, and it implies some ability to predict the outcome of the process through implementation of strategies designed to accomplish the desired objectives.

- *A managed process* embraces not only the fact that there are means to guide and control the process but also the implication that the process is someone's explicit responsibility. In other words, the process is not left to take care of itself.

- An extension of the qualifiers *planned* and *managed* is the idea that organization development is a *systematic process* based on a coherent body of principles, conducted by design, and carried out methodically. Moreover, the term *systematic* suggests unity in that each element of the process depends for its effective functioning upon every other element. This view of process connotes a socio-technical concept in which the distinct personality of an organization is a function of the relationships of its people and material. Social structures and behaviors are partially determined by the social structure and behaviors of the members of the organization. A systematic approach to organization development includes concerns for all aspects of the organization, importantly not overlooking people and technology.

- Change in all parts of the *culture* of an organization may be a major goal. Culture refers to the "feel" of an organization as perceived by its members and to the climate that determines the members' roles, attitudes, and relationships. Culture also includes the purposes of an organization, the values that support its functioning, the norms that regulate its behavior, the social interactions that characterize its operations, and its sources and modes of influence. Fundamental to change in culture is the matter of where influence exists and how influence is exerted: A cardinal value of organization development is the introduction of shared or distributed influence—based on the assumption that people will be more committed to objectives if they have participated in establishing them. Underlying this assumption is the belief that creativity and competence usually are widely distributed throughout an organization, regardless of hierarchical levels or job functions.

- Change in an organization's systems involves *methods and tools,* the artifacts of culture, that make possible an organization's operations. These universally are everything needed to get things done: systems of policies, procedures, and practices; organization structures and jobs; and facilities, material, and equipment.

• Change in *behavior* is a major concern. It is here that
behavioral sciences and technologies evolved from behavioral research make a strong contribution. Organizations are seen as
human systems; organization development, therefore, stresses improving human behavior and interaction on the premise that the
only real organization is the human system and that the material
components are merely the supporting mechanisms or tools that
help the human system function. Because of this emphasis on
human behavior, the concentration necessarily is on experiential
development rather than on purely intellectual exercises or head-
level education. People learn best by doing, and organization
development strategies are best carried out by working on tangible
problems rather than on abstractions—however fascinating they
may be. This behavioral science influence is evident in the view of
the organization as a social system composed of groups that
represent subsystems within the larger organization. These subsystems interact and take on values, norms, perceptions, and behaviors
that may or may not be conducive to cohesiveness and strength.
Organization development recognizes and capitalizes on the ability
of these subsystem groups to become stronger and to interact more
freely.

Although conceptual models illustrate elements and steps in
the time sequence of any change project, they usually also indicate
a particular bias toward collaborative and democratic problem-
solving. While most behavioral scientists tend to favor this kind of
commitment and process, it is important to recognize that there are
other ways in which change has been initiated and carried out—and
that to them can be applied advantageously an eclectic selection.

Stages in Planned Change Efforts

The Norwegian Institute of Personnel Administration, a
consulting firm, has successfully used a methodology of product
identification, project definition (in other words, terms of reference), data collection, issue identification and analysis, conclusions
and recommendations, implementation planning, management decision, implementation, and planning. In the industrial democracy
of Scandinavia, this method heavily involves both management and
employees in each step of the process. The major challenges often

are to bring in the two parties evenly, to build up common trust, and to obtain inputs from both employee and management representatives. The key to making such a change process work lies in including all the people within the organization—on a participative-group basis, shared at various hierarchical levels of the organization but within and among groups at each level. Thus the process remains rooted in group dynamics theory, and the means of carrying out the activities to meet objectives is designed around the interaction of groups. This emphasis on group participation springs in part from the belief that groups can be more effective than their individual members acting alone, that all of us know more than any one of us knows. Multiple perspectives and talents may be brought to bear in solving problems, setting goals, or implementing projects or activities. Furthermore, group rather than individual inputs are sought because the quality of the contribution thus may be more in keeping with the values of openness, authenticity, and candor. This is especially true of process activities pointed at communication improvement and conflict resolution. There is less implied threat in completely candid communication if it comes from group consensus, and both the quality and quantity of communication thereby may be increased.

It is essential, however, that these be real groups. A group in a social unit is defined as a collection of people with common purposes or interests, interdependent status and psychological awareness of each other, values and norms that regulate their behavior, and individual self-perceptions that collectively they are a group. Clearly, many aggregations of people do not constitute a group in this fuller sense, and much effort justifiably is expended in organizational development to introduce these attributions into an organization's members. When a number of individuals become a true group, the result can be unusual strength and capability and an effectiveness beyond that of independent or segmented effort.

Lippitt's Critical Phases of Planned Change

A perspective on critical phases of planned change is expressed by Lippitt (1973):

Diagnosis of the Problem. It is difficult to overstate the importance of diagnosis in the change process. In the same breath, however, we must observe that diagnosis generally does not stand as an end in and of itself and that in most cases it must be translated into a course of action for change before it becomes meaningful. The history of planned change shows that most change agents erroneously approach each problem with predetermined diagnostic orientation. Some of them invariably feel that the basic problem is bound to be either an uneven distribution of power caused by a faulty interchange of ideas—often defined as poor communications—or the result of poor utilization of resources. Such prejudgment should be energetically and conscientiously avoided. The available methods to collect data eclectically *with an open mind* represent a wide range of skills and approaches. In some instances, direct questioning may be the best way, but it often turns out that the best diagnostic data are a result of the relationships incurred in taking on the problem.

Assessment of the Client's Motivation and Capacity for Change. If change is to occur, it must come about primarily through the hard work of individuals within the group or organization. It is not enough merely to experience the discomfort of problem awareness: This awareness must be converted into a desire to change, and this in turn requires a readiness and capacity to change. In a community, for example, people will have conflicting desires—on the one hand, they want the advantages that change may bring, but on the other hand they do not wish to give up the known security and satisfaction they currently enjoy. The ability to recognize readiness for change and to cope with resistance to it requires considerable sophistication on the part of the change agent.

Assessment of Change Agent's Motivation and Resources. From a practical point of view, it is important that the initiator of change clearly assess his or her ability to help in a particular situation. If the change agent decides that special skills and knowledge may be helpful, he or she then incurs a further responsibility for defining what reasonably may be expected from the change project in order to secure the proper supplementary resources.

Selecting Progressive Change Objectives. After diagnosis, the movement toward the final goal is a sequential process that requires a number of subgoals or objectives; therefore, the place to begin must be chosen in terms of overall strategy. The starting point frequently is referred to as the leverage point. This may be a person, persons, or group especially salient or accessible to change and therefore receptive to communication. Alternatively, we may think of the leverage point in terms of patterns of behavior or in terms of a crisis in the organization such as the dropping of a product line or increased competition.

Choosing the Appropriate Role for the Consultant as Change Agent. Tied in with the selection of leverage points is the selection of the helping role: In what way should the change agent relate to the problem? One way is to make possible new connections and reorganize old ones. Another role the change agent often assumes is that of an expert on procedure or method. The change agent may, for example, provide the group or organization with techniques that will enable it to find out more about itself through the use of self-survey or self-education devices. Consultants acting as change agents may eclectically advise different behavioral training or a program of supervisor training. There is a danger, however, that in the American culture, where self-improvement is so valued, follow-through procedures may become ritualized and sterile unless they are accompanied by means of obtaining fuller understanding of motivation. Collateral to the role of the change agent is an advantage in creating a special environment for change. Sometimes the environment or the organization culture can provide a direct impetus for change within the organization. In other instances, it may be no more than a necessary background for promoting the effectiveness of other change forces.

Maintenance of Change. Once it has started, maintaining change may involve the inception of an ongoing training program in an industry or the freeing of communication so that feedback may be made available to policymakers. It is conducive to establishing lasting change in one part of a system if other related parts are prepared for change. Everyone needs support while working for change, and this usually can be provided if the person desiring change is assured that experimentation in new directions is useful and desirable.

Termination of a Helping Relationship. Problems surrounding the termination of the helping relationship are more profound

in cases in which it is used directly to effect change, as in the case
of psychotherapy. Even in large social systems, the resolution of
both parties' dependency needs may be a matter of concern. Generally, there is likely to be considerable dependency in the early stages
of the relationship, and, if the client thereafter comes to rely heavily
on the change agent for support and guidance, the termination is
apt to be an awkward and painful affair.

Bennis's Program of Planned Change

Yet another viewpoint is presented by Bennis (1963), wherein
he identifies eight of the traditional programs, as he calls them, that
are used to take advantage of people's knowledge and influence
change:

Exposition and propagation programs assume that knowledge is power. It follows that men and women who possess "truth"
will lead the world.

Elite corps programs grow from the realization that ideas by
themselves do not constitute action and that a strategic role for
leaders is necessary for the implementation of ideas (for example,
getting scientists into government).

Human relations training programs are similar to the elite
corps idea in that they attempt to translate behavioral science
concepts so that they take on personal characteristics of people in
power positions.

Staff programs provide a source of intelligence within the
client system, as in the work of a social anthropologist advising
military governors after World War II. The strategy of the staff idea
is to observe, analyze, and plan rationally.

Scholarly consultation programs include exploratory inquiry, scholarly understanding, discovery of solutions, and scientific advice to the client.

Circulation of ideas programs build on the simple idea of
inducing change by getting knowledge, and thus a sense of options,
to the people with power and influence.

Development research programs have to do with seeing
whether an idea can be brought to an engineering stage. Unlike
scholarly consultation, development research is directed toward a

particular problem, not necessarily for a particular client, and it is mainly concerned with implementation.

Action research programs, the term coined by Lewin (1951) and further development by Thorsrud and Emery (1964) and Herbst (1974), undertake to solve a problem for a client. Action research is generally similar to applied research except that in action research the roles of researcher and subject may be reversed, the subjects becoming researchers and the researchers engaging in action steps.

Confrontation and Interfacing

While these various approaches may differ in objectives, values, means of influence, and implications for action, all of them tend to concentrate on the use of knowledge to gain some socially desirable change. Bennis (1963) makes one important criticism of all of these methods: Each of them makes the assumption that knowledge about something means that there will be some resultant intelligent action or change. This notion has been demonstrated in both research and experience not to be true. In change situations, there usually is an element of experimentation, risk, insecurity, challenge, and fear. This is not to say that these attributes are lacking in the programs evaluated by Bennis (1963) but rather that there always is a need to recognize that change involves confrontation. Such confrontation will involve the counterstrength of courage, whereby meaningful and maintained planned change can take place in four different areas: *knowledge* (cognitive or conceptual understanding of the change), *skill* (the incorporation of new ways of performing through practice of the changed behavior), *attitude* (the adoption of new feelings through experiencing success with them), and *values* (the adoption of a rearrangement of one's beliefs). Confrontation also must be combined with searching and coping, which tend to eliminate from confrontation the extremes of pleasantry and recrimination.

Confrontation implies a facing up to the tangled web of relationships, issues, problems, challenges, values, and potentialities that invariably hang like a curtain between the entities into which people are divided or into which they divide themselves. This is called interfacing. Unless each involved entity—conceived here for the sake of clarity and brevity as being singularly or collectively an individual, a group, an organization, or a political or natural subdivision of man-made society—sincerely tries to penetrate this curtain, communication rebounds in sterility. If confrontation is only tolerated and neither processed nor acted upon, change ends in a cul-de-sac. If a change idea is received and processed in a rational mind but not acted upon, neither individual nor society benefits. But if the elements of receiving, processing, understanding, and acting upon are present in an exchange of ideas, the first elementary step has been taken in the search for interfacing.

Thus, interfacing is an aspect of the search for the self and the other. Buber's (1964) concept of the I-Thou relationship exemplifies the essentials of the search for comprehension and understanding between persons. As he stated, "Existence cannot be possessed but only shared in." The energizing effort to reach out to the other releases one's self in the process. Such a search is the essential linkage between confrontation and coping. Once this search is underway, the act of coping becomes a common attempt to solve, to know, to emphasize, to understand by means of equitable change in whatever relationship is confronted. This essential step in interfacing, together with confrontation and search, produces a dynamic interaction in which the reality of change is faced, resolution produced, and action effected. suffice it to say that whatever concept of change is contemplated, a variety of planned change efforts is taking place all the time between, for example, parents and children, teachers and students, administrators and subordinates, and federal government and state government. Although strategies for planned change have advantages and disadvantages, there are certain common elements to any planned change effort (Lippitt, 1973):

Advocacy is the first of these elements. In any change situation there needs to be some individual, group, or collection of groups advocating a change and willing to persevere in an attempt to secure such a change.

Time is always a factor. One of the naive assumptions some of us have made is that change can be effected quickly. We now know differently from our failures and successes. Whether you look at an individual working for two years with a psychotherapist, a group change that takes place over several months, or an organizational change that takes seven years, it is not difficult to grasp the reality that change seldom occurs overnight.

Collaboration and *cooperation* between certain power forces in the systems are essential to making change permanent. The support of the power persons early in the advocacy of the change may not be necessary, but if change is to be sustained they will need to be affected and involved, and their cooperation must be secured.

Systems approach casts an eye on the interrelationships between subparts of an organization, and these interrelationships must be understood and accounted for—or the change effort will end in futility.

Interrelationship of changes to other aspects of a system's behavior must be accommodated. An isolated change cannot stand alone; it must be phased into and related to other activities within the total system.

Emotion and *rationality* inevitably are elements of change. People need to be involved with their total being—which includes their feelings, sentiments, and values—or the change will not be accepted, or tolerated, or supported. In this era when many planned changes are brought about by temporary groups and systems— battling a housing development, resisting a new interstate highway, protecting trees, influencing the battle against pollution, making organizations more participative, or getting government to listen to citizens' complaints—many efforts fail because implementation and "follow-through" are ineffective. This usually is the weakest part of planned change.

Much, if not most, of the change within organizations is unplanned, but a creditable amount is distinctly attributable to conscious efforts by managers and professional change agents. In such instances, the organization becomes a client and the organization's system is viewed as a client system. We here illustrate this point with a case study of a Norwegian bank.

Initiation and Planning of an Organizational Change Effort

Norway has had a number of exceptionally creative and active research workers and research institutions supported by the central employers' and workers' organizations and by individual companies. As new elements in the theory of organization appeared, various research projects showed a relationship between technological factors and the social, psychological, and health conditions of the workers. The sociotechnical systems approach resulting from pioneering research done in British coal mines and, as well, the theory of autonomous work groups made an important contribution to the theory underlying the Norwegian experiments with new forms of work organization (Thorsrud and Emery, 1964). The Institute for Industrial Social Research was established at the Technical University in Trondheim in 1958. Under an agreement effected in 1962 among the Institute for Industrial Social Research, the Norwegian Federation of Trade Unions (LO), and the Norwegian Employers' Association (NAF), a Cooperative Board was established; known as the LO-NAF Cooperation Project, it acts as a permanent supervisory council. This project is based on a collective agreement among the central organizations regarding the terms under which experiments with new forms of work organization could be performed.

In the initial phase of the LO-NAF Cooperation Project, the influence of representative institutions in organizations was evaluated. Researchers looked into past experiences with cooperation committees and with other formal means of giving workers representation in the top echelons of companies in Norway and elsewhere. The conclusion reached in 1964 was that, on the whole, worker representation at the top level cannot be regarded as an effective means of achieving industrial democracy (Thorsrud and Emery, 1967). Somewhat unexpectedly, the central organizations comprising the LO-NAF Cooperation Project agreed with this conclusion. A second phase of the project consisted of a number of field experiments in which the research workers, in cooperation with members of the work force and management representatives, tried to develop new forms of organization that would give the individual employee greater direct participation. Such redesigning was aimed at formulating and providing for six psychological job demands (Gulowsen, 1971): variation and meaning in the job, continuous learning on the job, participation in decision making, mutual help and support from fellow workers, meaningful relation between the job and outside social life, and a desirable future in the job other than through promotion and increased income.

To this the cooperation board added the criteria that the rate of increase of productivity in companies participating in the experiments should be at least equal to the general average of increase in similar companies. Four companies were selected for the field experiments, and the general conclusion reached was that—in comparison with traditional forms of work organization—the experiments showed that it was possible to create (1) a high degree of personal commitment on the part of an organization's personnel and (2) opportunity for the development of their skills and competence by organizing the work so it could be accomplished by autonomous groups (Langseth, 1979).

Only a limited number of experimental projects were accepted as part of the LO-NAF Cooperation Project. This was unfortunate in that it made many people believe that a great deal of specialized assistance was needed. In later years, the focus of the Norwegian experiments changed; in the latest experiments emphasis has been placed on the action approach that had been an integral part of the theory of Norwegian experiments from the start. The action approach implies that research workers should not have a fixed preconception of the intent of the redesigning process but should let all those involved decide its course through repeated trial and error. Several companies have been experimenting without research assistance, either on their own or in cooperation with others (Langseth and Werring, 1979). In Norway, experiments have also been made outside industry. Under the auspices of the LO-NAF Cooperation Project, experiments have started, for example, in hotels and commercial banks and on ships, which demonstrates that the principles governing experiments in industry can also be applied to other sectors of the economy.

As the first such experiment made in the banking business, a change effort was planned and actually implemented in the Christiania Bank and Kreditkasse, the third largest commercial bank in Norway at that time, employing around 2,500 people. The change effort was first tested in one branch office and later implemented in five others using these phases:

Initiation. The change effort of this bank was inspired by the movement toward action research and with the deep conviction that satisfied employees do a better job, that staff involvement is critical for an effective change process, and that the quality and motivation of the human resource is the why and wherefore of success in any service industry. The personnel director decided to involve a consultant as a change agent. This consultant was given the mandate to develop an approach to organizational change that covered thirty branch offices. In making this decision, the personnel director was supported by the head of the Staff Association, a Norwegian bank's "white collar labor union," which has more legislated rights than are typical in the United States. For example, the elected president of the Staff Association is by law a member of the bank's board of directors.

Selection of Instruments. The change program used had been developed as part of a Ph.D. program in Switzerland (Handelschochschule, St. Gallen), and the process instruments had been pretested in Swiss organizations before being used by this Norwegian bank. The necessary data collection tools were adapted from this earlier procedure, and training programs were designed specifically for the employees of the bank to be involved in the process.

Preconditioning the Client. Staff Association representatives and management at different branch offices were approached by the change agent to determine whether their organizations were interested in and ready for a change effort. Without their approval, the change agent could not present the planned change effort to the employees. With this accord in hand, it was feasible to describe what was planned in a two-hour presentation to all employees in the branch offices. This included the purpose of the change effort, a suggested plan for how to proceed, the necessary time commitment, possible pitfalls, and the hoped-for outcome of such an effort. This done, the employees were asked to give a confidential vote on whether they wanted to go ahead with the change effort. Two thirds of them had to vote yes before the change effort could proceed. The result was affirmative.

Problem Identification and Description. Two task forces were elected among and by the employees. Task Force One was asked to identify and describe important issues, based on a survey.

Task Force Two was requested to come up with recommendations for improvement in the areas identified by Task Force One. The members of each task force were given twenty hours of training by the change agent during bank hours, primarily on group dynamics and on how to achieve problem identification and description.

Data Collection. The rationale for a predesigned questionnaire was explained to Task Force One, and task force members were given the opportunity to add to the questionnaire issues they felt were important. The original questionnaire was based on the illustration of job satisfaction shown in Figure 2 (Langseth and Werring, 1979). The questionnaire—as modified by members of the task force—was sent out to all employees and managers, together with a memorandum signed by the personnel director and by the head of the Staff Association. This survey was confidential, and more than 85 percent of the employees returned the completed questionnaire to the change agent in a preprinted envelope. The results were processed by the change agent, using a special computer program that analyzed and presented the data in a swift and meaningful way. These data were given to Task Force One, which then had to do all the necessary analysis to describe the issues so identified.

Feedback to Employees. A summary report of the survey results was prepared and presented to all employees without comment. Several issues were identified: (1) inadequate human resource management, (2) lack of communication between management and employees, (3) inadequate management skills in middle management, (4) insufficient staff participation in decision making, and (5) insufficient airconditioning in the bank building.

Recommendations to Management. Based on the analysis done by Task Force One, the members of Task Force Two started a series of meetings in which they came up with recommendations for solving the identified problems. They held more than twenty meetings within three months. Their recommendations to management included an implementation plan based on priority and cost. Top-level management, advised by the change agent, reviewed the task force's recommendations and quickly encouraged rapid implementation. Employees of the bank were asked to assist management in implementing the changes recommended.

Figure 2. Job Satisfaction: A Definition.

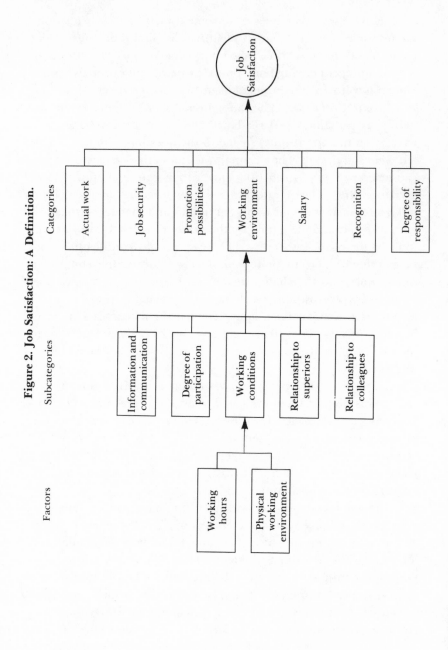

Evaluation. It was agreed by all concerned that after two years a new questionnaire should be issued in order to see whether the actions taken actually solved the problem identified and to identify new problems that might have arisen.

General Learnings. A change such as the one implemented in the Christiania Bank and Kreditkasse certainly offered the employees an increased level of participation in and influence on decision making. The basic rationales (Langseth, 1979) for effecting this change were highly practical. Employees, who live every day with the problems management needs to solve, are often quite capable of identifying and describing root causes. But the tendency is to underutilize employees' skills and resources, even though in most organizations such increased participation in decision making would be job enriching and would afford opportunities for personal growth and deeper loyalties. It was the positive experience of this banking organization that the employees greatly enjoyed working together in solving their own organization's problems and that they had a lot of insight and skills of which management was unaware. As a matter of fact, their issue identification and description, as well as their subsequent recommendations, were worked out as competently as they would have been by any external management consultant. In addition, several serious problems in the branch offices were solved, and the efficiency and effectiveness of these branches, including the employees' job satisfaction, increased as a result of the changes effected.

A negative experience, not altogether unexpected, was that middle management personnel at first slipped into a situation in which they were squeezed between top management's endorsing and pushing the project and lower-level employees using it as an opportunity to criticize. Weaker middle managers, of course, were distinctly more threatened when confronted with employee critique than were the good middle managers. Not surprisingly, therefore, the lack of management skill in some of the branch offices was identified rather specifically as an outstanding deficiency. The task force recommended sending all the middle managers to an appropriate training course. In the beginning, not a few of the middle managers were evidently disturbed by this and other recommendations, but after a year of living with the new perspective gained from additional training, the employees perceived a dramatic improvement in branch office management.

The change process involved in this case study can be characterized as rolling a snowball uphill. But through the commitment of time and investment in training, many of the organization's problems were lessened and, as a consequence, the organization's efficiency, effectiveness, and work environment were distinctly bettered. It was demonstrated, therefore, that, as conducted, this particular change process was indeed valid. It was not accomplished, however, without the whole project occasionally hanging in the balance. The experience, though successful, provided a sharp lesson: Such a change process must be wholeheartedly and universally supported. If the motivation does not exist whereby the change process is strongly and equitably endorsed by the vast majority of top managers, middle managers, and employees, then the organization is not ready for change and, therefore, its members are incapable of working together toward a common goal. And the danger prevails that without such motivation the change process easily can lead to a frustrating situation in which problems are created or magnified rather than solved. This is why—to many change agents of considerable experience—a change process is seen as irreversible, something that is much less difficult to initiate successfully than to stop harmlessly. In summary, therefore, it is unwise to initiate a change process until the organization is entirely ready for it. And, equally important, one should never start a change process when there is no clearly foreseeable positive effect on the issues identified as needing resolution.

Initiating and Planning a Change Effort at the World Bank

A change process was planned and implemented at the World Bank that was an amalgam of the different approaches just discussed, borrowing in particular from the experience of the Christiania Bank and Kreditkasse in Norway. The Administrative Services Department—with the assistance of a change agent who had been involved with similar change efforts in Scandinavia and Switzerland—established in October 1983 a support group that served as a steering committee for the ADM Strengthening Project.

This committee of eleven persons included technical specialists, process observers, consultants, and pertinent management personnel, and they were to be responsible for process consulting and implementation and technical assistance. The support group, thus composed and mandated, was first obligated to plan an organization change process. In order to clarify the support group's understanding of the complexity of such an undertaking, a detailed Project Evaluation Review Technique (PERT) chart was devised that encompassed in its flow all the pertinent and intended activities, the actions to be taken and by whom, and the people to be involved and how.

With this chart before them as a guide for in-depth consideration of all aspects of the change project, the members of the support group promptly determined that it was imperative to establish a common terminology that would be used by everyone to be even remotely touched by the projected changes; this would allow everyone to develop a similar broad understanding of the process whereby such changes were to be effected; and it would *precondition* management and employees alike with respect to how time consuming and complicated the process was likely to be before completion. It was decided also that the most effective way to achieve these understandings would be to distribute widely an informative brochure that told in plain language what was about to take place, explaining such things as the purpose, objectives, project overview, resource groups, role of consultants, and phases of implementation. Although thus comprehensive in nature, it was necessary in addition to provide room for future flexibility by making it explicit that the published presentation dealt with only one way among many in which the process could be conducted.

In the revealing and searching exercise of preparing the text for this brochure, the support group found it essential early on to secure among its own members three major areas of agreement: why the project was being undertaken and what they hoped the organization would be like after the project was completed; the respective roles and authorities of management, the steering committee, and the task forces that were to be formed; and, not to be taken lightly, the governing timetable. Thus, the writing of the brochure caused members of the support group to reexamine again and again the substance of the anticipated changes, the scheduling of actions, and the need for and use of extensive resources to support and facilitate the planned process. The refining of their thinking and, therefore, the planning, was penetrating and continuous. As a result, when finally published, the Strengthening Project brochure quickly became the foremost planning tool throughout the department. It is helpful here to discuss the change project as set forth in *ADM Strengthening Brochure*.

Objectives of the ADM Strengthening Project

As envisioned by the support group, the purpose of the ADM Strengthening Project was to initiate within the Administrative Services Department a process of improvement that would ensure that its services would be delivered in an appropriate, efficient, and economic manner by personnel working under conditions that would give them job satisfaction and opportunity for personal growth. This boils down to bettering effectiveness and environment. In the light of this purpose, the support group hammered out these objectives:

Revitalized Organization. This objective foresaw reorganization, if necessary; additional personnel, if needed; and specialized training for people, as appropriate.

Delivery of Superior Services. This concept envisioned an attempt to achieve zero level for avoidable errors and delays, as well as concurrently achieving responsible economies.

Enhanced Work Environment. Here the committee had in mind more effective communication, increased nonmanagerial involvement in and responsibility for decision making, broadened delegation of function and accountability, an accepted and fair reward system, and movement toward happier contacts between employees and their managers.

New Concepts to Improve Functioning. These would include management information and time-reporting systems; means to monitor and assess delivery of administrative services, with nonmanagerial participation and shared responsibility; long-term and strategic planning; and greater use of technology.

Improved Customer Relations. This objective sees the World Bank itself as a customer of the Administrative Services Department and anticipates greater awareness of and response to this customer's needs. It also encompasses involving this customer in planning and evaluating the delivery of services—and more open, more frequent communications.

The work groups of the change project themselves deserve explanation. The deputy director of the Administrative Services Department represented front office management, which ultimately was to be responsible for the ADM Strengthening Project; in that capacity, he headed a support group comprised in large part of people selected from the Administrative Services Department's own Personnel and Administrative Department. Together with the consultants, this support group provided, among other things, a liaison person for each task force, and it supplied external and internal resources, advice, tools, direction, and essential participation and counseling; thus, it coordinated the project department-wide in order to ensure smooth functioning of the change process, established a forum for reviewing at critical stages the efforts and progress of each task force, and made rational feedback available to those concerned. The task forces, operating at division level, were manned by both managerial and nonmanagerial employees; the chairman of each task force was elected by its members. Each task force was charged with reviewing for its division the working environment and the services provided to the banking establishment of which it was a part, even to the extent of creating within itself subgroups to study narrow issues and minor functions. These task forces were authorized to conduct such reviews when and as they thought best, but almost universally the guidance provided by the support group was used and found to be helpful. As guidance, each task force was given the *ADM Strengthening Brochure,* which had a separate section entitled, "One Possible Way to Conduct a Review."

Planned Phases of the Change Project

Now let us briefly describe the important phases in this World Bank change project as they were planned and shared with all participants at the beginning of the ADM Strengthening Project:

Preconditioning. After identifying the objectives and preparing the brochure, the director of the department and the members of the support group were to meet with all the division managers and senior employees in an extended conference at which the *why* and *how* of the proposed change process would be thoroughly explained. This done, they were to meet with nonmanagerial employees for the same purpose—division by division. At these conferences, the change process was to be pictured as an opportunity for the employees to wield influence over their own working conditions, and it was emphasized that nonmanagerial involvement was *sine qua non* for success. Most of the employees came to perceive participation as job enrichment.

Setting up Task Forces. Each divisional task force was to consist of approximately ten persons elected by their peers according to three rules: at least three members were to be selected from among the professional employees, three members were to be representatives from the support group, and the division chief had to be a member but could not be elected chairman. Group training was to be instituted promptly for each task force; and shortly thereafter each task force was to assume semi-autonomous responsibility for devising its own rules of procedure, reviewing background summaries, and setting up a work plan.

Collecting Data. Comprehensive and confidential questionnaires were to be distributed to all involved in the change process, together with preprinted, sealable envelopes in which the completed questionnaires could be returned to the consultants. Fundamentally, this procedure was directed at determining the nature and scope of the situation with which the support group was about to contend—the broad cultural and functional panorama of who, what, when, where, how, and why. The questionnaire would ask each respondee to relate his or her personal concept of the reason for the existence of his or her division or unit and an expression of personal understanding of what was being done by that division or unit to carry out that particular role. Each respondee also would be requested to explain his or her own role in some detail and to describe the activities that that role entailed. Questions would be posed in an attempt to see whether each employee knew the division's product and who received it as a user. All of these data, factual and subjective, would be reduced to volume statistics on resources, people, relationships, perceptions, and available skills.

The support group also was to obtain information concerning procedures and the flow of the work that went into every activity and every product. In addition, quality criteria and standards for output were to be examined and productivity assessed. Against this background data, the customers—the internal users of services and products—would be queried with respect to evaluation of the appropriateness and value of what they received from the Administrative Services Department.

Environmental factors were to receive close attention. In particular, people, both from their own viewpoint and from the viewpoint of the bank, would be looked at with respect to their skills, preferences, career prospects, appreciations, languages, experience, and motivations. The important management factors— organization structure, formal reporting procedures, management style, delegation, controls, performance measurement, reward system, recruitment, and selection processes—were to be analyzed in depth. The nature of the various work assignments, including such characteristics as uniqueness, interdependence, variety, job design, task organization, equipment, space, light, noise, and ventilation were to be probed.

The social aspects of peoples' relationships with the bank and with each other were to be critically examined. An effort was to be made to learn about social and work interactions, personal sentiments, attitudes toward cooperation, and shared likes and dislikes. The support group was to delve into such external negative factors as the constraints imposed by standard, typical bank routines and lack of job mobility.

An attempt was to be made to compare the information gathered through the questionnaire with that obtained in other, more or less similar organizations; and for each service provided by the Administrative Services Department, alternative sources within and without the bank itself were to be proposed and evaluated.

Data Analysis. A study of the wealth of information in hand probably was expected to reveal that opportunities did exist for development and improvement—as well as bring to light some areas that had no problems at all. Chances to effect betterment were

to be considered issues of importance. As an example, one such issue
may have been insufficient awareness on the part of users of services
not only that the support and assistance received were essential but
also that they emanated from the Administrative Services Department. With respect to these services, some users may have held views
and assigned priorities distinctly different from those of the supply-
ing division. Some available services and activities may have been
no longer needed by anyone, while others that were urgently
required were impossible to obtain. Chances to reduce costs, improve quality, and apply alternative ways of doing things or to use
more up-to-date technology may have been revealed, as well as
better ways to use human and material resources and means of
improving personnel morale and level of motivation. The desirable
sense of relationship to and participation in the bank's mission may
have been shown to be flawed in some ways, and internal communications may have needed revamping.

Planning Action Based on the Data. Following analysis by
the task forces, the identified issues were to be sent to the support
group for review and confirmation. Once the issues were so recognized and accepted, the task forces would be expected to develop
strategies, propose alternatives, and prepare recommendations that
would take into consideration cost, complexity, benefits, and time-
tables. These recommendations were to be sent to top management
for approval. After having decided what to implement, the task
forces would be informed in writing; they would then develop
detailed, short-term, and multiyear action plans. These plans would
be reviewed first by the division manager and second by the support
group before being forwarded to top management for final
approval.

Implementation of Action. Division management would be
responsible for implementing actions that were short term and not
constrained by lack of resources. Approved multiyear plans would
be integrated into the division's long-range work program.

Evaluation. Implementation of all plans was to be evaluated
after twelve months. If needed, new task forces were to be established
in order to assess the effected changes and to identify new issues
arising out of such changes.

Reflective Comments

It became stridently evident that in initiating and planning this change effort two widely distributed sets of guidelines were essential. One was a continuously revised blueprint for action. The other was an explanation of what was being attempted and how it was to be done. Both of these documents proved to be invaluable to inculcating an appreciation on the part of top management and to keeping the members of the task forces from drowning in the somewhat fluid process.

A major concern was avoiding the rocks of skepticism and the quicksand of apathy, these negative emotions being particularly prevalent among the middle managers. Our tactical motivators relied on enthusiastic project leadership, ample and believable organization-wide communications, and indelible commitment on the part of members of the task forces.

CHAPTER THREE

How to Involve People in the Change Process

We have found that the best people to solve complex organization problems are those who face them every day. We also know that it is the people in an organization who can implement or block needed changes. Involving them in problem diagnosis can result in reaching better solutions—and ones that work.

Let us mention two of the relationships between change agent and changee that are discussed in the current literature on organization development.

Perspectives from the Literature

Decision-Making Style. As a practical guide for managers, the Center for Creative Leadership offers five distinct styles for use in deciding when and how to involve others in decision making (see Figure 3). This decision tree is functional in that it allows a problem to be stated succinctly and then permits a manager to select yes or no answers in working his or her way through each question until he or she ends up with one of the five decision styles. Such a choice of decision is critical to success in most change efforts.

Exercising Personal Influence. Planned organization change involves at least one person exercising personal influence. Steele (1982) discusses four broad categories of influence that can be used

Figure 3. Decision Styles Flow Chart.

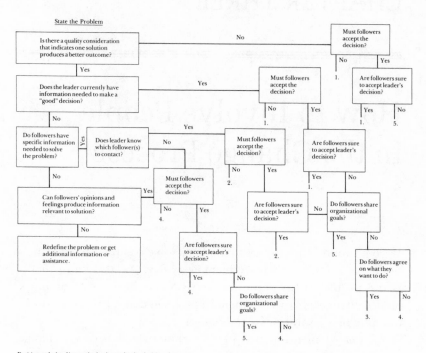

State the Problem

Decision style 1:   You as the leader make the decision alone.
Decision style 2:   You seek information and then decide alone.
Decision style 3:   You consult with selected individuals, then decide alone.
Decision style 4:   You consult with your entire group, then decide alone.
Decision style 5:   You share the problem with your group, and you all decide mutually what to do.

Source: Amended and printed with permission of the Center for Creative Leadership, Greensboro, North Carolina.

in a practical way by managers, contingent upon the situation at hand: *rewards and punishments, participation and trust, common vision,* and *assertive persuasion.* This hypothesis proposes that individuals have an influence profile and develop a consistent pattern in the way they try to bring others around to their view of reality. As an example, one person might be strong on rewards and punishments coupled with assertive persuasion, whereas another person might consistently try to achieve the same end by combining common vision with participation and trust. A planned change may require the use of all four categories, each at a different time and for a different reason. The change agent and, as well, the client, must use care and skill in selecting and asserting influence styles throughout a change process. An important decision in preparing others for and involving them in a change process, therefore, is that of choosing appropriate influence strategies. We have summarized in Table 3 when each of these influence styles is likely to be effective, but the change agent must weigh whether any given style at any given moment is congruent with present and future influence strategies. There simply is no one best way to use influence in bringing about change; therefore, the art of adapting an eclectic freedom to a given situation is quite helpful.

Managing a Task Force

Organization problems sometimes need to be dealt with outside the formal hierarchy. The use of ad hoc groups for problem solving is found at one time or another in most organizations. In the last few years, the most often discussed of these types of problem-solving groups have been the quality circle and the task force. In planning the change project at the World Bank we could have used either of these two formats, and the reason we chose the task force mode deserves attention.

There is little doubt that the widespread use of quality circles contributed significantly to the dynamic growth of Japanese industry and, not at all to anyone's wonder, the format has subsequently received worldwide scrutiny and imitation. It is predicated on the accepted and commonplace philosophy that an organization's own people are its most valuable problem-solving resource within a limited scope of work and environmental considerations. Quality circles involve small numbers of workers who meet regularly on company time in an effort to develop feasible ways to maintain quality production and waste avoidance. One can imagine that eventually this process finds new problems hard to come by, with a resultant replowing of a great many well-worked furrows. Nevertheless, we are led to believe that in Japan more than nine million workers regularly participate in the one million quality circles with which they are affiliated. Since Honeywell and Lockheed first initiated this concept in the United States in a culturally modified

Table 3. Four Categories of Exercising Personal Influence.

Category	Likely Effective Use When:	Likely Ineffective Use When:
1. **Rewards and Punishments** Prescribe goals and expectations Evaluate behaviors Provide incentives and pressures	• you control something needed • you have the power to give and they want direction • you don't care about a long-term relationship • you can evaluate and reward shortly after actions	• they see rewards and punishments as illegitimate • you can't reward • you can't assess whether standards are met • they have a strong need for independence and will reject rewards and punishments
2. **Participation and Trust** Personal disclosure Test and express understanding Recognize and involve others Collaborate to get identification of others' goals with yours and yours with theirs	• you need their active commitment and involvement • you will not be around to administer conditional rewards and punishments • you must rely on someone following your wishes on their own • you need real collaboration • they will resent your attempt at one-way influence	• you are the best decision maker • their real commitment is not needed • you only have one course of action and won't be influenced • you are expected to be the expert and not collaborate • their interests are not best served by collaboration
3. **Common Vision** Generate a shared identity (common values, interests, style) Articulate exciting possibilities Use energy-raising nonverbal behaviors (eye contact, animated movements, alertness)	• you must influence a number of people to make what you want to happen occur • there is a common set of values and interests • you want commitment to carrying out a purpose where how this is done is not important • others identify with you	• they mistrust your intentions or values • you are not held in high regard • there are no clear steps they can take to achieve the common vision and they don't know what to do
4. **Assertive Persuasion** Proposing ideas, suggestions on how to proceed or on concepts to be accepted Reasoning for and against when you present arguments	• you are seen as the expert • you are perceived as objective and not selling something that doesn't relate to their needs • you are the only source of information • you know enough of their situation to speak of their needs	• they have a strong need to be independent • you and they are competing • they have strong opinions of what they should do • they don't feel valued or appreciated by you • you patronize or are condescending

form, a number of other large corporations—among them General Electric, Boeing, Westinghouse, and General Motors—have dipped their toes into these unfamiliar waters. The chief motivation for using this format in both Japan and the United States almost certainly centers on increased morale, from which, it is hoped, other desirable qualities will emanate. But critics abound, and even in the Orient, rigid conformity to structured group norms in perpetuity have made it difficult for some new members to be accepted into and to participate effectively in a quality circle. This is an instance of a solution creating new problems. It has been demonstrated without question that nowhere are quality circles a do-all panacea for organization quandaries, and many companies outside Japan are convinced that—because of their industrial relations history, their organization structure and hierarchy, or their basic culture—an ever-sitting committee in time produces no more than committee-bred decisions of decreasing value.

Characteristics of a Task Force

A task force, American style, somehow is a different breed. In order to gauge the nationwide use of task forces for planned change, the Industrial Conference Board surveyed 247 companies and found that, although a multitude of reasons and purposes were reported, the responses broke down into three categories of nonexclusive task force objectives: study, analysis, and recommendation; measurement and evaluation; and action planning (Rush, 1974). Thus, the task force is a temporary group of appointed or elected persons who are brought together on a full- or part-time basis to examine a problem, recommend solutions, and sometimes evaluate and implement the solutions thus recommended. Task forces may be composed of representatives from several organizational levels or areas. Their purpose is to bring differing perspectives to bear on the group's task. A group of persons from differing levels but in the same functional area, such as manufacturing or marketing, is called a *"vertical slice."* A group of persons of equivalent rank but from different organizational areas is referred to as a *"horizontal slice."* A *"diagonal slice"* includes persons representing various functional areas as well as several hierarchical levels, while a *work family* task

force is composed of individuals who regularly work together—
including, as appropriate, the unit head. Among all of these, there
is one cardinal rule: When the problem is solved or cannot be
solved, the task force disbands. Within these dimensions, task forces,
including the work family groups used at the World Bank, may
have nine characteristics:

Problem Orientation. The task force may diagnose, resolve,
and evaluate specified situations within its organization and within
the boundaries of its charter. More often than not, decisions are
reached by consensus.

Change Orientation. A task force must be adaptable to
changes proceeding around it. The external environment may
change, the organization may face a new crisis, or budgets may be
cut or increased; these kinds of things may affect the problem as
originally delineated, alter political support, or increase or diminish available resources.

Systems Orientation. The task force must have an understanding of how its organization works internally and of how the
organization interacts with its environment.

Multidisciplinary Focus. Complex problem solving, especially in the area of organizational change, demands input from all
relevant disciplines. The task force membership must include or
represent the range of expertise necessary to solve the problem, and
it must effectively integrate the inputs of diverse specialists.

Horizontal and Vertical Organization Relationships. The
classic chain of authority in an organization is not the basis of task
force membership. Members who are knowledgeable about the
problem to be solved are chosen from different levels and functions
within the organization. They should be interested in reducing the
problem, able to work with others in the group, and credible to
other members of the organization who must live with their
recommendations.

Planning, Delegating, and Monitoring. A plan that breaks
objectives into manageable components must be prepared by the
task force. Individuals or subgroups must be given lucid and
measurable goals, deadlines, and resources and sufficient time in
which to do the work. Their activities must be monitored and
coordinated by the task force or its representatives.

Innovation. Solving complex organization problems seldom involves walking a well-traveled path; it almost always requires a novel approach. The task force members may need to learn—and help others learn—the art of managing innovation.

Finite Duration. A task force necessarily must have a beginning and an end to its existence. Once the solution has been introduced and demonstrated as effective, the task force should be disbanded. If ongoing diagnosis or supervision is required, people other than task force members should be put in charge.

No Optimum Size. If a task force is too large, it will lack critical mass with which to become cohesive and, for that reason, group process issues may not be resolved. If it is too small, it may lack sufficient members and, for that reason, the appropriate disciplines or skills with which to resolve the problem. We have found that between eight and ten regularly attending members is just about the right number and that—if an organization-wide change is contemplated—the office of the chief executive must be represented on the task force.

Workings of the Task Force

Now that we have defined the standard task force (there may be exceptions, for good reasons), what does it do? This is something a manager should know. When a task force is responsible for overseeing change, large or small, it must undertake in prescribed order five distinct "tasks": (1) define the group's mission, goals, and objectives; (2) collect and analyze data and define by diagnosis what needs to be changed; (3) select among feasible courses of action and generate an appropriate way to bring about change; (4) plan and recommend activities, processes, scheduling, and implementation that will produce such change; (5) review, evaluate, modify, and reevaluate what the group has recommended. During each of these phases, the task force must be concerned with the time, funding, and resources allowed by the organization's managers, seeing itself as a cooperative, problem-solving group that can constructively handle dissent among its members and that takes full advantage of the contributions that can be made both inside and outside the organization. With these obligations firmly in mind, a task force must organize itself by calling upon four of its members to assume vital roles:

Chairperson. He or she must be able to help the task force define and select the problems that are related to its assignment; see that all members of the task force participate fully and are able to express their views without inhibition; keep the discussion on track; clarify and summarize the progress toward the task force's current or overall objective; and help maintain a cooperative and productive climate, including dealing effectively with disruptive behavior. The chairperson may perform some of these functions at times and places other than in the meetings of the task force. The planning and organizing of work between task force meetings often is supervised and coordinated by the chairperson, and his or her networking with influential members of the organization is a primary role. The chairperson has an ultimate responsibility to know what is going on, to communicate information, and to understand how circumstances and events may affect the work of the task force. Meetings must be held frequently enough to keep members of the task force up-to-date with alterations in outlook and role and with the group's progress toward achieving its purpose. The chairperson must be sensitive to conflicting loyalties created by drafting members of the task force from various parts of the organization, and he or she must avoid becoming too closely involved with any one function of the task force's performance (Ware, 1981).

Group Facilitator. This member helps the task force improve its functioning by examining substance and process and making observations thereon that may facilitate group problem solving. This role requires a certain amount of analytic detachment.

Recorder/Reporter. This person notes the sense of all discussion, including commonly understood major problems uncovered, issues at stake, agreements reached, decisions arrived at by consensus or vote, and recommendations distilled therefrom. The recorder/reporter delivers summary accounts to management, writes down the actions to be taken and the due dates for implementation of the task force's recommendations as approved by management, and may be assigned by the chairperson to undertake the task of follow-up.

Resource Person. Usually a specialist in his or her own right, this member of the task force helps the group marshal particular facts and contributes to the discussion from the viewpoint of one field of expertise, such as finance, strategic planning, technology futuring, demography, or the organization's own business perspective. The resource person, with essential sensitivity for others, never reflects discredit upon any other task force member. Under his or her direction, a team of specialists may be assembled to sit with the task force by invitation.

Training to Alleviate Problems

Problem-solving task forces are benefically used in a variety of settings to help diagnose, introduce, or evaluate organization change. In some situations, however, a task force is inappropriate, as, for example, when one person acting alone is the best decision maker, when the real commitment of the members is not needed, when there is obviously only a single course of action to be taken, when one person is supposed to be the expert, when collaboration with others is not in order, and/or when the best interests of potential members of a task force are not served by their participation.

Quite real problems also may be generated by the use of a task force (Ware, 1981): Conflict may occur between the members of the task force and the members of the organization who are responsible for the existence of the problem the task force is assigned to resolve. A meeting of the task force may become a battleground on which are fought out long-standing intra- or interdepartmental differences. For many reasons, there may be inadequate commitment of the members' time and energy. Members of the task force may seize an opportunity to score points with top management or to enter into problem solving with secret agendas; they may not know each other well, or they may harbor hidden hostilities—both of which circumstances may make it difficult to share a sense of purpose. In general, however, task forces are functional and productive when properly established and directed. Our experience at the World Bank turned out to be an example of successful use of task forces; thus, for the practical guidance of others, it may be helpful for us to deal with how to involve, prepare, and develop managerial and nonmanagerial personnel for this kind of assignment. Let us start with some of the things that can be achieved by training:

Behavior Objectives. Mager (1973) has written a simple, programmed learning book that will teach a manager in about an hour how to write out "behavioral objectives," a statement that shows what a trainee will be able to do at the end of the training, under what important conditions, and how well. This concept helps put rigor into training programs and assists in evaluating whether a need for training has been correctly judged and met.

Innovative Problem Solving. Imagine being given the problem, "What else can be packed into a tea bag other than tea?" In practice, dozens of answers can be generated, but they almost all fall into four categories. The first category deals with the question literally and includes herbs and novelty toys. The second attempts to conjure up new uses for the bag and includes use as a paintbrush for children and as a burn dressing. The third undertakes to envision a structural change in the bag itself and includes acting as a sweat absorber and as a container for insulation material. The fourth category sees different uses for the material used in the construction of the bag and includes diapers and curtains.

Innovative problem solving is an exciting process for task force participants and often offers insights into problems that other methods fail to achieve. We did not use this methodology as a part of our change process at the World Bank, and by this oversight we missed an important opportunity. The truth is that people involved in helping to resolve organizational difficulties need to develop skills and techniques in innovative problem solving.

The following example of an innovative problem-solving method was adapted from the Center for Creative Leadership, Greensboro, North Carolina and used with their permission. The first step in this method is to meet with the client before the session to identify: (1) the problem statement—a brief headline definition of the problem, (2) the background of the problem—essential details, not all details, and (3) solutions that have been tried. This rehearsal of problem statement and analysis often helps the client to be concise and to the point when the group meets. At that time, the four rules for brainstorming form the foundation of the actual problem-solving session: (1) Suspend judgment—throughout the session, the facilitator should remind the group of this rule. (2) Seek high quantity of ideas—when idea flow dwindles, the facilitator should reenergize the group by seeking a new direction from the client. (3) Freewheel—to set the tone for freewheeling, risk taking with ideas, the facilitator should encourage the client (during the preliminary meeting) to be speculative and to demonstrate an open attitude toward all kinds of suggestions. (4) Cross-fertilize—the facilitator can increase cross-fertilization by interjecting at appropriate times the question, "Can anyone build on that idea?" or similar phrases. In addition to ensuring that the brainstorming ground rules are followed, the facilitator is responsible for the general structure and energy level of the session.

The process involved in this problem-solving technique includes the following steps and tools:

1. Problem statement and analysis

   - Ask the client to give a headline statement of the problem and to write it on the chart.
   - Ask the client to give essential background information.
   - Allow participants to ask questions in order to clarify the problem. Be careful not to let the questions become too specific; the participants do not need to become experts.

2. Immediate ideas

   - Ask participants to give any solutions they have already thought of; this will get out the more obvious and convergent ideas. Write these ideas on the flipchart.
   - Check to see if the client wants to pursue any of these ideas; if yes, skip to 5.

3. Problem restatement

   - Ask the client and group to restate the problem from as many perspectives as possible; write them on the flipchart in headline form.

- Elicit clarifications and elaborations of any problem restatements that are not self-explanatory. Encourage participants to transform, "break set," and search other "worlds" for analogous problems. Remind the group, if necessary, to concentrate on transforming and restating the problem, not on generating solutions.

4. Idea generation

- Have the client select a problem restatement and then state why it was selected.
- Ask the client whether he or she has any ideas on how to implement a solution to that particular problem restatement.
- If the client has no ideas in this area, ask the group for ideas that would solve that problem restatement. Remind the group of brainstorming rules.

5. Idea sorting

- Ask the client if any of the ideas generated thus far are possible solutions to his or her problem.
- State reactions to such an identified idea(s) first as a paraphrase and then as an itemized response—first listing several positive aspects, then indicating concerns.
- Have the group generate ideas to try to reduce the client's concerns.
- Observe that ideas become possible solutions when the client expresses no immediate concerns.
- If time permits, allow the client to subject another problem to the same process.

6. Conclusion

- Give client the flipchart and all worksheets.
- If additional ideas occur to a participant after the session, pass these on to the client.

Task Force Process. There always is an urgency to be concerned about the process followed by a task force. A process consultant, as well as the members of a task force, should be well acquainted with the variety of roles people tend to assume in group action. Wedgwood (1967) categorizes these roles into three major groupings: (1) *Blocking roles*—aggressor; blocker; withdrawer; dominator; recognition seeker; topic jumper; self-confessor; special interest pleader; playboy; devil's advocate. (2) *Building roles*— initiator; opinion giver; elaborator; tester; clarifier; summarizer. (3) *Maintenance roles*—tension reliever; compromiser; harmonizer; encourager; gatekeeper.

The World Bank: How We Involved, Prepared, and Developed Others

One day at the World Bank, we found a poem pinned to an office wall. It concerned the unwilling doing the impossible for the ungrateful. This thought, so foreign to the people with whom we were working, made us glad that our client was the World Bank. Not everyone, of course, will enjoy such an advantage of working with willing and cooperative people, but it should be remembered that the process we followed had much to do with the prevailing attitudes toward and receptivity for change.

The project manager and the internal change process consultant completed the project work at Harvard Business School. It was decided to supplement the project team with a management consultant, who, in addition to contributing in his area of expertise, would be responsible for logistics. This reinforced project team discussed the change process in depth with the top managers of the World Bank and secured their concurrence with the purposes, procedures, resources, and timetable of the project. The project manager, who was the deputy director of the Administrative Services Department, was told to make the project his primary activity; to make this practicable, his personal management time was somewhat freed up by the appointment of two assistant directors for the department. Then, a detailed memorandum describing the project was distributed to all managerial employees in the department, followed by two oral briefing sessions—the first for the ten senior division managers and the second for all other managers down to unit chiefs.

As planned, a support group was organized, with the selection of members based largely on technical, organizational change, and interpersonal skills—as well as on a sound knowledge of the department. We were fortunate indeed in these selections—and when we were unable to do much to relieve these people of any substantial portion of their ongoing day-to-day responsibilities, they gave generously of their off-duty hours. Later, an external change consultant, a training adviser, and a personnel officer also were brought on board. After the support team was thoroughly indoctrinated, we were able to proceed with the last stages of preconditioning, presenting the project's purpose, method, and schedule to division employees in groups of fifteen to thirty-five— and specifically asking for their help in making the project successful. In these meetings, the concept of task force participation was explained—first, that all the nonmanagerial employees in each division would elect nine of their peers or managers to serve with the division chief on a task force charged with diagnosing needed changes throughout the department; and second, that in this process any employee in the division might be called upon to sit with a sub-task force to study a particular problem. The votes were to be tallied by interested but neutral outsiders.

Over 85 percent of the employees in the department took part in these elections. It would be impossible for anyone to believe that everything everywhere went smoothly—and it did not. The situation was in part saved by the integrity and the high personal standing of the project manager within the department: He was known to be concerned, open, and genuine, and he was trusted. Nevertheless, as happens in almost all representative elections, there were complaints from a handful of employees whose candidates did not receive sufficient votes. And in one division, only 46 percent of the employees voted—which in itself was a red flag remarkably difficult not to notice and which represented a distinct threat to the entire project. Such a low response rate could indicate either acute disinterest or knowledgeable lack of trust. An inquiry routed via the informal influence network returned a guileless response: The employees in that division did not have much confidence in their managers and thus did not accept the likelihood of anything more than cosmetic change.

The project manager and internal change consultant arranged to meet quietly with small groups of these unhappy and more or less recalcitrant nonmanagerial employees and separately and alternately with their supervisors and managers. They absorbed the charges and countercharges, allowing steam to escape: So-called horror stories of the past were dredged up and relived, personalities were raked over hot coals of recrimination by both sides, lack of effective and lasting change was repeatedly cited, and an irreducible disbelief in the occurrence of change was manifested; but respect for the project manager was such that there was a slow movement toward at least *trying* the task force concept. Some of those most heatedly concerned wanted to be sure no supervisor or manager would serve on the task force; but well-guided, open discussion finally produced a consensus that such exclusion would lead to serious problems in implementation. Once again, ballot forms were distributed, and the discussion was allowed to continue without the presence of any member of the support group or any manager or supervisor.

The protracted conferences were emotion filled and exhausting to all who participated, especially the consultants; but they were also steadily therapeutic. Several minor crises were survived, essentially because of the strength of the process. One of these involved an exceptionally able and well-liked employee choosing to leave the room rather than approve the participation on the task force of any managerial person. Another squeeze point occurred when the unavoidable absence of the project manager was taken as a slight. In the end, however, the secretly cast votes in this division were proportionate to those cast in the rest of the department; the resultant task force, perhaps because of its traumatic birth, produced dramatic recommendations for change, all of which eventually were approved and implemented.

Each task force included up to ten members, and from this constituency were elected a chairperson and a recorder. A process consultant was assigned to each group, and expert resource persons were on call. Each perceived problem was shared with the entire group at a task force meeting—during which training was interspersed—and by consensus the members defined their purpose, set objectives, collected data, diagnosed situations and circumstances, generated solutions, and prepared action plans. In doing all this, they were fully aware that their recommendations would be subject to review and, as appropriate, revision by the support group. The chairman of the support group, the project manager, would discuss the task forces' recommendations with the senior managers of the bank, modify them if deemed advisable, then reroute them back to the originating task forces for reconsideration. It is important to observe that this procedure had two advantages: It enabled the modifications to be free of personality conflict, and it could be repeated as many times as necessary in order to reach agreement between the upper and nether levels of authority. This constantly revitalizing "yo-yo" action had the beneficial effect of constantly refining thinking throughout the organization until eventually the proposed changes were understood and accepted at all levels. In fact, in the bank only a very small number of modifications were found to be needed, but the refining was a useful safeguard.

As noted previously, one of the threats to the success of such a procedure was the presence on each divisional task force of the division manager, who was decidedly an authority figure to be apprehended in both the present and the future. This potential dominance and suppression was counterbalanced effectively by several means. The membership of the task forces, having been elected by their peers in each division, held a degree of power in their de facto representation of all the employees in the division, and the division manager could not be elected chairperson of the task force. Thus, since the process consultant was empowered and encouraged to circumvent managerial power plays of any kind and, being relatively independent of divisional politics as well as having ready access to the powers that were at higher levels, there was little compunction about cutting off a division manager's attempt to manipulate.

Despite the fact that many of them spoke warmly about the experience, some of the engaged managerial personnel undoubtedly felt that being compelled to share their role was an intrusion on their authority. A consequence of the election process, not altogether unexpected and thus a calculated risk, was that lower-level managerial personnel ended up being slightly underrepresented. However, the ratio of managerial to nonmanagerial personnel on the task forces demonstrated a palpable trust in the judgment and equipoise of the latter when it came to making decisions concerning changes in their own organization. In addition, a task force tilt toward those employees who did not bear a burden of organizational responsibility tended to avoid built-in managerial conservatism and opened the floodgates of less conservative thinking. In spite of these rather advantageous results at the World Bank, however, we recommend that, in similar change efforts in other organizations, the matter of participation by various levels of management be given careful consideration.

As mentioned previously, during the program on organizational change at the Harvard Business School, the project manager was able to add to his existing knowledge of and experience with organizational change by engaging in practical problem-solving case studies in an academic atmosphere. But this preparation for a change effort at the World Bank also had other advantages. For example, the real possibility of a dependency relationship developing between the project manager and his internal change consultant was avoided: By exposing both of them simultaneously to a variety of means and values, a common strategic perspective was achieved. The internal change consultant felt that by encountering a jungle of competition and achievement demands, of impersonal scrutiny by qualified teachers and trainers, of fine tuning of their plans and visions, they would develop a deep mutual trust and later would be able to approach situations in real life with greater shared understanding and appreciation.

The Training Phase

Training the Support Group. The responsibilities of these participants extended to preparing the members of the task groups for what they were to accomplish; acting as technical or process advisors collectively or individually, to each task group or component subgroup; reviewing the progress of each task group; and maintaining a high level of motivation and enthusiasm. It quickly became apparent that these responsibilities generated three distinct needs: The support group itself needed a senior process consultant, and for this role it called upon one of the authors. Because the employees in the Administrative Services Department represented more than sixty nationalities, the multicultural aspects of communications and interpersonal relations presented an exceptional challenge. We relied in part on the work of Gazda (1973) for training in this area. The process consultants needed refresher courses. To meet this requirement, we designed and implemented a two-day seminar in process consultancy that included summarizations of the latest literature, a number of analytical tools, and practice recognition sessions. Unfortunately, our training did not include sessions in displaying interpersonal skills, but we did become familiar with the ideal sequencing of such interpersonal skills when attempting to help a group or individual.

Gazda (1973) was helpful because he provided means to acquire skill in discriminating between several interpersonal expressions and in recognizing their relative presence or absence in utterances. These expressions include: empathy, warmth, genuineness, self-disclosure, respect, concreteness, immediacy, and confrontation. Empathy, for example, can be defined as "an utterance that shows the other person that he or she is accurately understood beyond the level he or she has expressed, that underlying feelings are identified, and that the content is used to complement the understanding of that other person's feelings and to add a deeper meaning."

Egan (1982) proposed that a helping relationship progresses in order through three stages and that if the helper or consultant fails satisfactorily to complete the first stage, then the succeeding stages are unlikely to be effective. In *stage one,* the consultant attends, listens actively, probes, and understands. He or she responds with respect and establishes a working relationship. In order to facilitate the client's self-exploration of a problem, the consultant must show empathy, warmth, genuineness, and concreteness. In *stage two,* the consultant helps the client see the problem in new ways, understand the need to take action, and set goals by which to manage the situation more effectively. Here the consultant uses the skills demanded by stage one, strengthening the evidence of empathy, introduces self-disclosure, immediacy, and confrontation, and assists the client in using alternate frames of reference. In *stage three,* the consultant helps the client develop a specific action plan and decide how to achieve the objectives of this plan. He or she encourages the client to implement the plan, giving support and direction, and assists the client in evaluating whether the problem is thus being managed more effectively. The skills required include all those used in stages one and two plus the preparation of action plans and the strong presentation of a support attitude. It should be noted also that Carkhuff (1980) earlier had prepared an interesting text and workbook on helping skills that used cartoons to illustrate the nonverbal aspects of this important part of any change process.

Training the Task Force Members. Fully realizing that it is unusual first to highlight a negative experience before relating a positive, successful approach, we would like to tell how we erred in attempting to design a training course for the eighty-five employees who would make up the ten task forces. A pilot course—a professionally presented off-the-shelf package—was tested three months in advance, using randomly selected people from the Administrative Services Department. The course introduced a logical approach to getting things done and put the participants through a series of artificial exercises, such as designing logotypes and undertaking traffic surveys, but it presented no visual models that would aid understanding, and it was almost devoid of training in the group process. In a word, the packaged course simply was not what was needed—and recognizing this negative was a first and perhaps necessary step toward deciding what *was* needed. Although it was anathema to experts in training procedures, this experience demonstrated that preparing such a large number of task force members called for an inductive rather than a deductive solution.

It was decided to set up a small ad hoc team comprised of two management training consultants and two members of the support team, supplemented by us. This dedicated group—charged with designing an appropriate training course—spent a full day inductively diagnosing the task force training requirements and preparing in outline form a training model. Two weeks later, the management training consultants had sufficiently elaborated this outline, created a satisfactory model, and developed specific training objectives. At this time, one of us was invited to critique this thinking and work and, as a result, by consensus, several important improvements were effected in the training course from which the task force members would so greatly benefit. (In its final form, the course consisted of two days of training in group development skills, two days of training in project planning skills, and one day of training in effective communication.) A shorter but similar training course later was designed for the supernumerary members of subgroups created by the task forces; their participation in such a training course was enthusiastically encouraged by the members of parent groups. The innovative aspects of the training course included:

- Making all the skill-building sessions on task group process and individual behavior take place in real group time; over half the available time was spent on this.
- Working on likely task force situations rather than on artificial problems. Examples of this are: outputs of the division, choosing a chairperson, delineating task force norms and rules of behavior, refining the purpose of the task force, and preparing an action plan by which to undertake the work.
- Incorporating the task force process consultants into the training course, making them responsible for feedback in real time, and getting them to train the task force members, as a group, in group process. This had a dual benefit: It quickly legitimized the role of the process consultant and eventually got the real group process off to a flying start.
- Spacing the course modules so as to get assignments completed before the next phase of training.
- Focusing on task force training—rather than on the needs of individual members of the task force outside the context of the needs of their group.
- Presenting the knowledge sessions in short lecturettes.
- Sharing information gained from other task forces that were floundering with similar group process problems, including any innovative processes or solutions that these other groups developed.
- Keeping the training fast paced. (The mild complaint was that the sessions were not quite long enough.)

A formal structure for the networking of the chairpersons of the task forces did not come about until we were about five months into the change project; this occurred naturally as the chairpersons requested informal meetings for the purpose of discussing various issues. Now, however, looking back, we recommend that, in any change process of comparable scope, a networking structure be incorporated into the planning, for implementation at the beginning. And it should be noted that the task forces, contrary to our expectations, did not incur a felt need for our planned use of outside experts in specialized fields. One task force sought the technical advice of a geographer, another called for advice with respect to organization structure, and several of the task forces asked for technical consultation only as a means to resolve a choice between two feasible solutions to a problem. However, the great majority of the task forces used, formally and informally, experienced and knowledgeable resource persons already available within their divisions. Similarly, not a few task forces were able to do without the assistance of a process consultant and indicated such independence by handling the process feedback function on their own. This we had hoped for. The support group promptly became fully trusted and stood as an important source of stability. At one level, the support group did not do much more than be there, listen well, ask guiding questions, and provide encouragement; at another level, it served as a medium by which ideas were exchanged among the task forces. All in all, the preparatory training succeeded well in convincing the participants that change was to be effected as a thoroughgoing *process,* and that it would not be impossibly complex. Most importantly, perhaps, we were most victorious in transmitting the belief that the workability of the change process depended almost entirely on the commitment and applied skills of *all* the participants, but particularly those who were nonmanagerial in status.

Reflective Comments

Involving and preparing others to participate in this change effort quickly became an all-hands evolution that called for early and simple expressions of ideas. One basic aspect of the preparatory training was to encourage everyone to see the change project as an occurrence in their "real world." Top management obviously was a first priority group, and from there the familiarization was happily extended downward so as to encompass almost the entire employee list of the institution, including many people who would not directly participate in the change process but for whom to *know* was better than to *guess* what was going on.

One tactical skirmish engaged in and won was that of securing for the project manager sufficient time to carefully plan the procedure and to estimate the resources required. It took many man-hours to bring members of the task forces to effective readiness, and their processing of issues was somewhat pedestrian, but the time investment paid off in the identification of the *real* problems and the *workable* solutions—and in the depth of sincere interest in implementing and fine tuning those solutions.

A deep and abiding concern, however, was that the planning somehow failed sufficiently to incorporate middle management into vital roles and functions in the change process.

CHAPTER FOUR

How to Identify and Choose Opportunities for Change

We have attempted to describe broadly how the change process at the World Bank was planned and how we preconditioned the people at the bank for the parts they would play in bringing about appropriate change. It may now be advantageous to illustrate in greater detail the procedures of data collection and analysis, how possible opportunities for beneficial change were isolated, and the methods of decision making.

Data Collection and Analysis

Organization diagnosis is defined differently by different practitioners and theorists in organization behavior. To us it is an analytical process of identifying and measuring the relevant and valid variables of organization effectiveness and efficiency—both qualitatively and quantitatively. We have briefly discussed qualitative diagnosis. Obversely, to the extent that is feasible, organization diagnosis needs to be measurement based—starting with a scientific, quantitative reading of the state of the organization and its direction of movement. This manner of measuring the way an organization is currently functioning can provide a sound basis for diagnosis, and such diagnosis becomes a foundation on which to implement a change effort.

As every married couple is aware, the interrelationships of even a dyad can be complex and offer a surprising number of variables. A larger number of people, organized for a reason understood by all, can provide a tremendous array of data to those who want to know, a panorama of significant information. At best, however, the most intense delving reveals only a tiny fraction of all there is to be learned. This is why organization diagnosis has been likened to looking into a room through keyholes, each keyhole presenting a different perspective of what is going on inside the room. Even so, the volume of information that can be drawn from most organizations in itself presents a dilemma of sorts. Because of limited time and resources and because of personal and professional biases, diagnosis compels application of a reasonable restriction on the kind and level of information gathered and on the depth of subsequent analysis. And diagnosis alone is never an ultimate objective—it is only a means of gaining insight essential to creating improvement strategies in some mode other than proceeding blindly; a change project undertaken without an appropriate diagnostic framework is not all that different from navigating without a compass. In pragmatic outlook, then, diagnosis is important because it increases the probability of steering a proper course, of addressing the predominant issues and applying the correct interventions.

Diagnosis breaks down into three components. *Data generation* involves the forms in which the data are gathered, the frequency with which they are collected, and the methods used to get them in hand. *Data organization* involves a means to handle the amount of data collected, an efficient storage and retrieval system, and a concept of order and precedence for collation. *Data analysis* involves first integration and interpretation and then sound evaluation and judgments.

Isolating Beneficial Change

Two fundamental methods of collecting information for diagnostic purposes are interview/observation and the questionnaire. The former tends to be more believable and interesting, although it is not of greater validity; the latter is more easily recorded, aggregated, and stored. Usually, both means are employed, but, for our purpose here, let us briefly concentrate on how the questionnaire normally is used.

At an early stage in a change effort, a questionnaire instrument is completed by all available members of an organization or of that part that is under study. This typically is done in monitored groups of twenty-five to fifty persons who can be given time off from their work assignments; sometimes this number of people is assembled during off hours. The process ordinarily is administered by someone from outside the organization so as to both give the impression of impartiality and confidentiality and ensure these conditions in fact. The form of and future access to the data so generated are described to the respondents prior to their completion of the questionnaire, and they are told when and how they will be given an opportunity to see and discuss the impersonalized data with their supervisor and other members of their work group. For many respondents, completion of a questionnaire under these circumstances may be a first exposure to an organization improvement effort, and such active participation in itself produces familiarization with and a favorable attitude toward a change project.

Those completing the questionnaire are informed that no individual will be identified as to his or her response. Thereafter, however, work group members—that is, a superior and subordinates—do have access to the impersonalized data generated by that group; and any supervisor is entitled to examine aggregated data generated within his or her area of responsibility. Thus, a department head receives data in two forms: first, data summarizing the responses of immediate subordinates; and second, data summarized for the entire department. The frequency with which data are collected differs with the nature of the information sought and the stability of the organization system. The more stable the organization, the less need there is to collect data.

Once the means to store data and to efficiently retrieve it is ensured, one of two options can be exercized with respect to collation. All data that has to do with a particular issue can be combined, or all the data can be organized according to source. The former obviously is preferable where the objective is to produce summary statistics concerning a particular issue; the latter is appropriate if the objective is to examine response patterns across areas of specified source, to study responses within designated target groups, or to compare relationships among selected areas of concern. The rationale for data analysis may be the tracing of strengths and weaknesses throughout the organization system, the identification of causes of certain conditions, or the matching of corrective methods with aptly fingered problems. In any event, the collecting and analysis of generated data precedes and, in part, influences the isolation of opportunities for needed and helpful change and the selection of appropriate interventions.

Solutions to a great majority of today's pressing organization problems that cover only those issues related to structure—or to structure and strategy—are seldom adequate or complete. Every organization is a unique blend of change variables: systems, style, structure, skills, staff, strategy, and something we call shared values (Waterman, Peters, and Phillips, 1982). These seven variables—all beginning with the letter "S"—can be combined into what is called the 7-S Framework (see Figure 4). This model, sometimes referred to as "The Happy Atom," was used by several of the task forces engaged in the change project at the World Bank and served as a useful conceptual tool for the support group and top management. It is, of course, an assertion of the belief that productive organizational change is something more than interactions among structure, objectives, and strategies.

The 7-S concept is predicated on six ideas. Foremost is the idea of a multiplicity of factors (seven here so far, although there may be more) that influence an organization's ability to change and that dictate the proper mode of such change. The division is somewhat arbitrary, but undeniably it has the merit of acknowledging the sheer complexity to be identified in research and of segmenting the tangled skeins into manageable parts. The model conveys the notion of interconnectedness of variables. It has been observed that failure or only partial success blights nine out of ten thought-to-be carefully planned change projects. Our educated guess is that those nine are failures in execution, a result of slighting one or more of the organization variables. Just as a

Figure 4. 7-2 Framework (Modified).

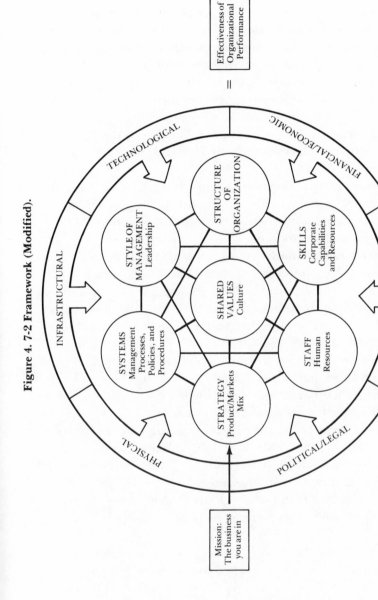

Source: Modification of the 7-S Framework originally developed by McKinsey and Company (1981). Adapted by Peters and Waterman (1982).

logistics bottleneck can cripple a military strategy, so too can inadequate breadth and depth of diagnosis make a paper tiger out of the most sincere attempt to bring about change. It is quite significant that the model possesses no starting gate, no implied hierarchy; this obviously means that any one of the variables, or any combination, might be the driving force for good or bad in an organization. The mission or business of the organization colors each variable, and the prevailing environment casts sunlight and shadow with fickle consistency. What then are these variables that are so important to every organization but that in the absence of enough competent diagnosis wholly lack superordination among themselves?

Shared Values. These are recognized aspirations and assigned degrees of excellence, written or unwritten, that go beyond the conventional, formal statement of organization objectives. They are the conceptual foundation on which the organization stands, and they provide the azimuthal course on which it is moved by top management. Not unlike the fundamental postulates in a mathematical system, these shared values are a point of departure on which the system is constructed, but in themselves they are not logically derived. The ultimate measure of an organization's common ground, however, is not necessarily its logic but rather its usefulness. An illustrative metaphor is to compare shared values to parallel railroad tracks that simultaneously are restrictive and directional. There is a managerial challenge, of course, in defining, articulating, and communicating such values so that all the human elements see themselves mirrored in the organization's performance. If this is done efficaciously, a stability usually develops where otherwise there could be rapidly shifting organization dynamics. In most organizations, shared values are more or less subliminal, but research has shown that they are clearly evident in the regimen of the superior organization performers (Waterman, Peters, and Phillips, 1982).

Strategy. In this context, strategy is the art of devising and employing plans that respond to and counterbalance changes in the internal and external environment. Chandler (1962) was the first to point out that structure follows strategy. For the most part, strategy is a paramount consideration for the profit-seeking corporation, the studied game plan for scoring points vis-a-vis the competition, the controlling concern in most business decisions. But Chandler's (1962) hypothesis is by no means the be-all and end-all of organization wisdom; too many examples of monolithic, prestigious companies around the world are demonstrating that the mere existence of pristine corporate strategy does not ensure excellent execution. It is illustrative that a large percentage of these corporate organizations are little maimed by reason of anything being critically wrong with either their structure or their strategy; the more likely cause of their inability to achieve set goals lies in one of the other variables of the 7-S model. Similarly—although such strategy can be perceived as being of somewhat tenuous assistance to the nonprofit and public sector organization—they too must weigh the effect of their stratagems against effectiveness and personnel morale.

Structure. In theory, structure divides functions, delineates pecking order relationships, provides a means of coordination, allows specialization, enforces integration and, perhaps exceedingly important, defines accountabilities. In days past, in business and industry particularly, the functional line invariably cleaved production and sales, and all was simplistically represented on an organization chart. There was almost universal acceptance of such principles as direct hierarchical relationships (one man/one boss), limited span of control, departmentalizing similar activities, balanced workload/staffing, and keeping commensurate all aspects of authority and responsibility. Experience, however, has shown us that size and complexity are dimensions that become critical in terms of structure. At a certain level of volume, numbers, and complications, a functional organization—which is dependent upon frequent interactions among all activities—commences to break down. As the number of people or branches or missions increase arithmetically, the number of interactions required to make things move smoothly ahead increase geometrically (Waterman and Peters, 1980). When any organization passes a certain benchmark in growth today, it must decentralize proportionately if it is to continue coping.

These developments have produced a relatively new structural component: the matrix. In concept at least, this is an attempt to reconcile the realities of organization complexity with the imperatives of managerial control. Unfortunately, the two-dimensional matrix model is intrinsically too simple to capture any real situation, and any spatial model that really does encompass that situation ordinarily is incomprehensible to the unaided mind. In terms of pure and virtuous structure, however, the matrix does have one well-disguised asset: It calls attention to a central difficulty, the omnipresent problem of exercising emphasis and coordination so as to make the whole thing work—that is, how best to distribute tasks. The challenge lies not so much in trying to comprehend all the possible measurements of organization structure as in developing the ability to focus on those measurements that are currently vital to the organization's upward evolution—being always ready to refocus as the crucial dimensions shift. General Motors' restless use of change of structure—most recently the project center, which directly led to its effective downsizing—is a case in point. At the World Bank, the change project demanded that the members of the task forces, these mini-organizations being themselves matrices, refocus on the structure within the Administrative Department.

Systems. This term covers all the procedures and processes, formal and informal, that make an organization go, day by day and year by year. It includes, among others, systems for planning and control, capital budgeting, training, computerized banking, human resources information, and cost accounting. This variable in the 7-S model could well be the one most likely to be dominant. Ordinarily, the systems are the first place to look for reasons why an organization does or does not get things done satisfactorily. And fine tuning its systems is the least disruptive way to change an organization. For many kinds of organizations, a system of systems *is the strategy.* For banking institutions, the development and implementation of a superior account profitability system has been the key to consistent improvement. Another intriguing aspect of systems is the way they mirror an organization's state of health. To many managers, strangely enough, the word *systems,* if not somehow frightening, seems to have a dull, plodding, middle-management connotation even though relatively minor changes in one or more systems can powerfully enhance organization and managerial effectiveness—without the disruptive side effects that so often ensue from tinkering with structure and relationships.

Style. As articulated and attributed to organizations, style refers to distinctive, characteristic performance that is a reflection of managerial leadership. Restated, style is a perceived pattern of actions and, as such, it is manageable. Literature dealing with organization development has but recently considered style to be an "at risk" factor, yet style is the dress of managerial thinking; it is so often the man and it so often appears in other garb when the dominant personality changes, and, perhaps inevitably, it as quickly betrays the overly strong as the overly weak. It is a nascent weight in the scale of today's organization effectiveness that is but adequately circumscribed as the right words in the proper places, the proper action at the right time. It much too frequently occurs that a management team is capable of thinking up to a towering, misplaced style. Top managers, as well as the public, have always sensed an organization style and its inherent gamble; the difficulty in handling it as a variable in the 7-S model is in measuring how it is received by managerial and nonmanagerial employees or associates on the inside and by the multitude of opinion holders who judge from the outside.

Skills. Rather than having to do with the master plumber or the proficient computer operator, the term *skills* here refers to the expertness and adeptness of the organization itself under the guidance of its managerial leadership. Skills are those attributes that characterize an organization, the basic things it does exceedingly well: IBM and customer service, Proctor & Gamble and brand management. Skills is a variable that is equal among the software elements of the 7-S model (style, systems, and staff are the others), and yet it probably is the most illusive and intuitive in terms of management. It comes into prominence when it is recognized as wise or necessary for an organization to revamp, adjust, transform, and adapt (Waterman and Peters, 1980). An appropriate metaphor for skills is to liken it to the ability of a seasoned small boat handler to so mind the helm as to sail close to the wind or to keep a course in a buffeting gale. So we refer to the subtle capabilities and reserve resources of will and innovation that make an organization especially adroit at continually responding to change of any sort in its environments (Waterman and Peters, 1980). We are talking about something above and beyond commitment to people, although organization skills absolutely must originate with people. We are reaching farther than merely seeking a higher average intelligence quotient among employees, although no one can deny that organization skills are immensely aided by smart people. Perhaps most important, skills can be seen as an intensity of organization perspective that permits it to maintain an appropriate "fit" among the other six variables. A bank or engineering firm, for example, that lacks the skills to forestall a misfit of systems with strategy could more or less achieve disaster. Can such an undesirable variance be detected before a stage of crisis is reached? This undoubtedly would be one of the difficult and intriguing issues to be faced at the World Bank by the support group and the task forces.

Staff. Here we look at the people in organization. Demographics, age profiles, sex, and nationality are examined in each function of the organization. Human resources should be reviewed for upgrading, succession, and career planning at each level of the organization. Selection, placement, and promotion may be impacted by the market place, technological needs, and the legal requirements for equal employment opportunities. Such special requirements for personnel also are closely related to the mission, products, and services of the organization.

To many people, it seems difficult to see the difference between staff and skill in the 7-S concept. Staffing is often treated in one or two ways. In the mechanistic manner, we can talk about salary systems, performance appraisal approaches, benefit schemes, personnel rules and regulations, and the like. At the developmental level, we talk about motivation of staff, morale, training, coaching, career planning, and the growth of individuals.

Several cogent ideas are incorporated into the 7-S model. For example, an organization is affected by many factors simultaneously; there is no single factor that alone creates an organization block. All of the seven variables somehow are interconnected and progress with one requires as well attention to all the other six. Similarly, failure in an attempt to implement any otherwise valid strategy with respect to one variable usually is due to inattention to the other variable. None of the seven variables necessarily is more important than any other; thus, if a critical variable should be revealed, it is made so by a situation. All of the variables are subject

to the macro- and microenvironments by which the organization is
or may be affected, including economic, political, ecological, soci-
ological, and psychological influences. The variables also mirror
the current stages of growth of individuals and groups within the
organization in all positions and at all levels of the hierarchy. For
an organization such as the World Bank, the international economic forces and balances have a direct influence on all seven
variables.

For the benefit of the task forces, the planners of the ADM
Strengthening Project developed a diagnostic tool that makes
practical the use of the 7-S framework. The approaches embodied
in this comprehensive guide—for each of the variables in the 7-S
model—include areas of inquiry, establishing what the diagnosti-
cians are looking for, data sources, and methods of data collection.
As is true of any diagnostic tool, however, the quality of collected
data and subsequent analysis gained from the 7-S framework
depends on the critical degree of managerial and nonmanagerial
involvement. At the World Bank, the latter was indeed heavy. It was
found advisable, and proved to be advantageous, also to include in
the diagnostic tool two important new fields of exploration: internal management processes and operating performance. These two
factors tended to compensate for the lack of output measurements
and evident environmental considerations.

Choosing Among Opportunities for Change

When organization diagnosis succeeds in uncovering one or
more unsatisfactory situations and reveals a likely cause or causes,
there usually is more than one way to eliminate or reduce the
problems. *Feasible* and *acceptable* solutions, however, are not all
that evident. In the change process, therefore, particularly when the
people in an organization participate in task forces, the art of
decision making comes into play. A thoroughly rational decision
will result in the selection of the best alternative, the implication
being that all the pros and cons of *all* possible alternatives are
carefully weighed. In practice, after one gets beyond the coin toss,
it does not work that way—all possible alternatives are not known
and, even if they were, human beings would find it impossible to

consider all such alternatives. This human limitation, therefore, is an effective bar to perfect decision making.

In the decision-making situation, Simon (1967) draws an interesting distinction between *economic* man and *administrative* man. The former is assumed in economic theory to know all the possible alternatives and their certain outcomes, and his choice among alternatives is made according to a system of values predicated on an economic referent, such as profit. More realistically, the latter knowingly or unknowingly reduces the perceived complexity of a problem to that level at which his knowledge and judgment limitations can cope with decision making. The typical decision maker is subject to such bounded rationality, since his or her capacity for solving complex problems alone is limited to the alternatives of which he or she is aware and since his or her perception of the situation may or may not be subjective, idiosyncratic, or individualistic. Although far from practicing instantaneous decision making, the task force—necessarily multiperceptive if not multidisciplinary—tends to modify the distortion caused by these human qualities.

Most of the writing and thinking about decision making is concerned with the business of selecting alternatives, but it is increasingly apparent that a wise selection of an alternative depends for success on the recognition, diagnosis, and generation stages of a decision-making process. It generally is believed that most individuals are poor decision makers (Simon, 1967); some research shows, however, that managers trained to move cautiously through the steps of a decision process, rather than following their natural inclinations, make superior decisions (Simon, 1967). From this conclusion, it is reasonable to assume that a *group* of decision makers also will make better decisions if it is guided by the concepts of decision theory, providing that a predetermined objective serves as a benchmark against which to measure the worth of an alternative and that there is a conscious accounting for the nature and quantity of ever-present uncertainty. Most organizations face more or less uncertainty in their environments; even the most logical, apparently best alternative at the time a decision is made will continue to enjoy those attributes only if the prevailing environmental circumstances remain unchanged.

The World Bank Experience

Why did we use decision theory in our change project? We made this choice primarily because each member of each task force was to play, however momentarily, the role of manager, and the decision theory school adamantly maintains that the ultimate, the most significant, the most prevalent function of a manager is the act or process of making a decision. The task force members were to be asked to step up from their daily bread stimuli and relatively ground-level perspective at the World Bank to survey the department—with all their everyday emotions and experiences intact—from the Olympus of an impressive change project. It was advantageous that they were made aware of what they were dealing with in the larger sense—a system—and that they understood rudimentarily the forces at play—the total environment. There is little reason to doubt that most of them came to see themselves, at whatever level they were employed, as representing a "discipline" in a multidisciplinary setting, that their convictions and sentiments were intrinsically valuable.

At the World Bank, the various groups engaged in the change process were given a working familiarity with decision theory as a means of honing competence and understanding of this function. The members of the task forces, particularly, were acquainted with the facts: that false expectations tend to surround a concept of rational decision making, that decisions seldom are based solely on an altogether emotionless ordering of information (although unquestionably this is a goal), that even within the ideally organized task force decisions will be a synthesis of collective background, status, and experience. In the light of this philosophical sense of counterbalance, members of the task forces were asked to determine issues from the substance of diagnosis and to select from their own generated alternatives what they considered to be the acceptable, feasible solutions—in a word, to identify the best opportunities for change and to plan a way to bring these opportunities into reality.

Obviously, these people were to be involved in a structured change process. Their choices were to be relatively great in the area of issues and problem solving and relatively small in terms of the procedures to be used. They could opt to use the 7-S model as a diagnostic tool and intellectual framework and be guided by a decision matrix. There was to be scarcely any limit to the reasonable support available to them upon request. But it was realized all too well that this planned change project was a first experience for almost all the participants and that despite general preconditioning the trust level between managerial and nonmanagerial employees was in places rather like quicksand.

Process Initiation and Task Force Elections

It was decided by the support group to have each member of each division task group (other than the division manager) be elected by secret ballot. The initial step in this election process took the form of a directive from the support group to all the World Bank people to be involved in the change effort. This communication first spelled out the purposes of the ADM Strengthening Project: to ensure that (1) services provided by ADM were adequate, efficient, and economical; and (2) the working environment offered staff adequate job satisfaction. Next, it specified the goals of the division task forces: to analyze (1) *what* the division was doing and for whom; (2) *why* the division was doing it; (3) *how* the division was doing it; (4) *how well* the division was doing it; and (5) *how the division could improve* the services it was offering in terms of adequacy, efficiency, and accuracy. Third, the memo specified who would be on the task forces: two fifths higher-level representatives, selected by staff; three fifths support staff representatives, selected by staff; and the division chief, appointed by management. Fourth, recipients of the memo were asked to elect the persons from their divisions whom they felt would best represent them on their divisional task forces. Each person was to vote for two higher-level staff members and three members of the support staff. Lastly, respondees were asked to fill out a confidential questionnaire consisting of three questions: (1) What are some of the things you like best about working for the World Bank? (2) To improve services to clients, what would you change in the way *your work group, your division,* or ADM as a department does things? (3) Please list what changes you believe are necessary to increase your ability to do a better job. Also make any suggestions about changes you would like to see, things that might be improved, special complaints you have, and so forth.

The election form and questionnaire, along with a pread-dressed envelope, were distributed simultaneously to all division personnel. Each division was represented by a different color of paper; it was thereby possible to monitor the rate of return without violating confidentiality. All involved personnel attended an hour-long briefing before completing the questionnaire. A generous amount of space was allowed for written replies, and, because the questions were open-ended, the respondees were under no restrictions when they raised issues and concerns. Thereafter, the elected task forces met weekly or biweekly for the first two or three months and then for the remaining four or five months were more or less on call.

Task Force Rules of Procedure

After the ten divisions completed their elections, a process consultant chaired a pilot task force meeting in order to demonstrate a way to select a chairperson and to demonstrate the establishment of rules of procedure. Each task force was free to adopt its own methods for accomplishing these two objectives, and the results were indeed varied. The former required somewhat more than ordinary time and effort for the simple reason that the ideas of managerial and nonmanagerial employees were interfacing. The latter—the markers and boundaries—were, of course, entirely self-imposed, and a few were interesting microcosmic studies in human nature. Following is a list of examples of task force rules of procedure:

- At the end of each task force meeting, an agenda for the next meeting will be established.
- The roles of observer and referent will be rotated among the task force members.

- The minutes of the last meeting should be distributed to the task force members prior to the next meeting.
- The division chief must *stand up* if he wants to speak in the capacity of division chief.
- Task force decisions require only a simple majority of votes, but minority opinions are to be attached to the report of the vote.
- At the end of each session, there will be a period devoted to discussion of individuals' problems.
- Our task force normally will meet at 11:00 A.M. on Tuesday in Room N-829, and sessions will be limited to two hours.
- Recorder is to have minutes from a Tuesday meeting to all members by 4:30 P.M. Friday.
- Each member of the task force will bring copies of all minutes to each session.
- The chairperson will ensure that all flipcharts are available at the meeting place.
- In cases of content issues, decisions will be made by a decision matrix; for process issues, resolution will be made by consensus from that session.
- If someone cannot attend a session, he or she should tell everyone that he or she will be gone and why.
- All sessions will be recorded but not transcribed.

The open-ended questionnaire worked well and the respondees—the task force participants—dealt with many issues and recognized numerous opportunities for change, the vast majority of them thoroughly valid and differing essentially in level of criticality. The data collected via the questionnaire became a substantial and sufficient information base for the change effort. Additional data that in the projected planning were to be furnished by the task forces actually were not given much attention—mainly because the issues identified by the questionnaire alone gave the participants more than enough grist for their mills. As a matter of fact, even with the support of a technical specialist from the support group, the planned supplementary data collection turned out to be too ambitious and probably would have been too complicated to be of value in the change project.

Analyzing the Data at Hand

Here the members of the task forces came face-to-face with transcribed survey data and, not unlike the blind men examining an elephant, were at first stricken with widely varying interpretations—except that the width and breadth of the project were startlingly plain to see. They were asked to engage in issues development and assessment—that is, to give form to opportunities for helpful change and to spell out the possible results if those opportunities were materialized. Preparing an implementation paper thereafter proved to be relatively less difficult. The ADM Strengthening Brochure was used extensively as a tool by each of the task forces. As an illustration, the important issues uncovered by one task force were: goals and objectives, resources, physical office environment, procedures and controls, organization structure, internal and external interface, image, communications, leadership, motivation, evaluation and rewards, strategies, grievance system, control of contractual services, work integration and efficiency, and miscellaneous. Some of the task forces grouped such issues according to the variables in the 7-S model. An elaboration by one task force of one of these issues—evaluation and rewards—resulted in this analysis with respect to action ideas and needs:

- Base rewards on performance
- Promote internally, train if necessary
- Strengthen attitudes toward work
- Give visible sign of credit for a job well done
- Give constructive criticism when counseling
- Provide clear performance criteria

In order to choose among opportunities and to develop a game plan for giving priority to options, we designed a set of decision criteria, although we recognize that there is no ideal list of criteria that can under all circumstances be infallible guidance for assessment:

Cost   Involves money, resources, sacrifice of other options, as well as energy, pain, side effects.

Benefits   Likely contribution the option may make to
                      solving the problem, reaching goal, success.
Feasibility   How likely is it that the option can, realistically,
                      under prevailing circumstances, be acted upon
                      so as to yield measureable results?
Control   To what extent is the group or individual (con-
                      sidering the option) likely to be able to harness
                      the resources, support, and opportunities so as
                      to implement *and* manage the option?
Timing   Given an analysis of prevailing circumstances,
                      when is the optimum time for implementation?
Time scale   How long will it take to achieve results?
Discreteness/
Interdependence   To what extent is the option something discrete
                      enough to be implemented on its own? To what
                      extent is it part of a complex interdependency of
                      other options whose success requires simultane-
                      ous or linked implementation?

We then also created the matrix illustrated in Figure 5. Such
decision-making tools were a part of the task force training and later
were used by most of the task forces as a means to achieve agreement
with respect to priority tasks.

During the process of setting priorities among identified
opportunities, the task forces came to realize that their perceivable
work load was greater than could be handled by so few people. This
led to a proposal for the establishment of a sub-task force structure;
as many as six such subordinate work groups seemed to be needed
by some of the task forces. This obviously was a decision for top
management to make, because whereas on the positive side there
would be worthwhile involvement of more World Bank personnel,
on the negative side there were the implications of increased cost
and disturbance and the need for extended coordination. Here the
positive was seen to outweigh the negative, and the task forces were
authorized to initiate as many sub-task forces as might be required
to do the job well. Some of the sub-task forces were reflections of
the 7-S model (see Figure 4) and thus dealt with: goals, objectives,
organization, and structure (shared values); procedures, standards,

Figure 5. Decision Criteria Matrix.

Option	Cost	Benefit	Feasibility	Control	Optimum Timing	Time Scale	Discrete	Rank

Rankings scale: 1 |___|___|___|___| 5   1 = not attractive as an option;   5 = attractive as an option.

contractual services, and work efficiency (systems); career development, job satisfaction, grievance system, and status of working
women (staff); planning, image, and leadership (strategy); and
communications (style).

The sub-task forces, however, did not float free. Each one was
headed by an appointed member of the parent task force, who was
responsible for recruiting up to six others to work with him. A
preliminary action plan had to be approved by the founding group,
a timetable was imposed, and progress reports were required.
Overall, a great deal of time and effort was contributed by the
members of these sub-task forces and, perhaps to someone's embar-
rassment, more than one of these subordinate groups turned out to
be more effective than their elected big brothers. Expansion of the
task forces in this manner did not altogether escape conflict. Could
a task force modify the report of its own sub-task group? Pride and
prejudice were involved and hotly defended. With Solomon-like
wisdom, the management group decided that in cases of friendly
disagreement, both positions would be forwarded to the arbitrating
support group for review. Eventually, all inputs to a task force were
coordinated and wrapped into a single report on which *all* the
personnel in that division were invited to comment. Again, these
new inputs were discussed and debated, denied or endorsed—and a
final report pinpointing opportunities for improvement was passed
on to the support group for the first but not necessarily the last time.

Once the matter of opportunities—the *what*—was stabilized
with the support group, a task force then had to buckle down to
preparing a corresponding plan of implementation—the *how*. This
was a different kind of task demanding a different kind of perspective, and it was somehow more of a challenge than what had
preceded it. Most employees in most organizations are readily able
to mouth what in their opinion "ought" to be done; only a few are
consistently able with equal facility to express a cogent and responsible course of action, such as the following action plan format:

1.   State the problem, issue, and opportunity.
2.   State the desired solution for improvement.
3.   Present an implementation plan, with action steps.

4. Estimate the number of personnel required for implementation.
5. Estimate the number of weeks required for implementation.
6. State a completion date.
7. Assign a priority level to this opportunity.
8. Identify an action indicator (an incident indicating that an action has been taken).
9. Identify an impact indicator (a measure indicating that implementation of this opportunity has actually made a difference).

Reflective Comments

The members of the task forces had to be supplemented by the creation of more than forty sub-task forces. Although not predicted prior to the need being perceived, this turned out to be a "good news" and "bad news" phenomenon. On the one hand, more employees became involved, and this drastically increased the base of personal commitment and provided even more penetrating analysis. On the other hand, the deliberations of both the task forces and their collateral sub-task forces consumed an enormous amount of time—little of which, surprisingly, was devoted to unadulterated wheel spinning but which nevertheless became a concern to those who found themselves hassled by middle management about getting their *other* work done.

An important but not altogether unacceptable concern for everyone was the greater cost, the wider disturbance of established routines, and the compulsion to extend coordination over many more people when the sub-task forces became a part of the change process.

CHAPTER FIVE

How Change
Should Be Managed

As we have said, large and rapid deviations from the status quo are
characteristic of our age, and organization management is mainly
concerned with the challenge of maintaining control of such
deviations. Thus, managerial coping with change, for the most
part, involves understanding and utilizing the human resources of
an organization. But are today's managers adept at perceiving need
for change and handling it once it is perceived? Unfortunately, the
art of planning and managing change has not had much opportunity to profit from hard case studies of failed attempts, and there is
a tendency to make somewhat vague, sanitized, and a trifle over-
blown conclusions from those instances in which even partial
success is achieved. This usually occurs because a little success is
trumpeted and the ghostly skeletons of near misses and utter
disasters are somehow thought best kept in their closets. As a result,
students, some practitioners, and an enormous proportion of unini-
tiated managers get the erroneous impression that the path of
change runs ever smooth, although it does not. But neither unwise
and errant managers nor their egg-smeared consultants undertake
to write about what went wrong and why, even though their doing
so undoubtedly would advance the cause for everyone. We are,
therefore, for the most part left to study the history and future of

the change process in terms of suspect reported triumphs and observable trends.

Future Trends in Managing Change

Our review of the most thoughtful projections of management responses, functions, and roles in the next few decades—by, among others, the Hudson Institute, Stanford Institute, Alvin Toffler, Espandiary, and *Futurist Journal*—has revealed significant trends: Authority will be polarized toward centralization and decentralization, while emphasis on distribution of accountability will accelerate. Meaningfulness of work life will receive ever greater attention. More flexibility in problem solving will be adopted, and there will be an increase in matrix management—getting the job done by putting the right heads together from any place in the organization. There will more frequently be creative integration of technical and human resources. The doers and the leaders of the informal influence network increasingly will be involved by management in planning and decision making. Stress and conflict management will be seen as signs of strength rather than weakness. Face-to-face interactions will diminish as new technologies of communication permit problem solving by widely separated participants. Innovations will be assimilated rapidly in managing and marketing—with more efficient use of procedures for identifying, documenting, evaluating, and spreading successful practices. Flextime, part-time jobs, and ad hoc assignments will become common as means of making more effective use of human energy and competence. An ever greater number of organizations—and not necessarily only those that are financially strapped—will practice the fine art of downsizing, learning to be lean without being mean.

All of these trends raise hurricane warnings of change— subtle perhaps, drastic possibly. As Toffler (1980, p. 25) stated: "There is nothing new about change, for it has always been part of man's history." And, of course, the fact that this old earth still spins and bears life tells us that mankind, as a species, has managed change—somehow. In the macrocosmic process of epic human survival, however, several civilizations have been utterly victimized by shifting fortunes; in the microcosmic twentieth century, thousands of organizations have succumbed because they could not cope with new perspectives, passively allowing proactive waves of competition and altered circumstances to wash them unwillingly onto the shoals of surrender, merger, or bankruptcy. We know now that ordinarily this need not happen, that modern management techniques provide the philosophy and tools with which, first, to anticipate the need for change and, second, to influence the way things are to be different.

Prescriptions for Organizations in Transition

How then, in essence, does an organization go about orchestrating its own change viability, smoothly adapting to new conditions, ever confidently moving toward greater maturity? What organizational physics and managerial pharmaceuticals enable us—people, that is—to stomach change appreciatively, to reject inappropriate meddling, to learn how to deal successfully with our fevered selves in kaleidoscopic environments that we did not ask for but have around us anyway? Let us, for starters, take a look at some of the more typical practices in managing people: *—) Creating behavior*

Involve All Employees in Planning for Change. Such participation helps people understand the change, gives workers confidence that management is not "trying to pull a fast one," and makes use of the ideas of those most intimately acquainted with the problems.

Communicate and Use Feedback. Providing an opportunity for a person to voice his or her objections in itself reduces opposition. Similarly, open discussion may reveal disguised reasons for being negative. For example, a person may balk at using a different piece of machinery because he or she will be moved away from a window.

Consider Effects on Working Environment and Group Habits. Particularly important to consider are such things as breaking up congenial work groups and disrupting commuting schedules and car pools. Know whether the proposed change will have a bearing on priorities and preferences for vacation time or assign someone to an older or younger age group, to a group with a higher or lower educational level, or to a group with incompatible standards of conduct.

Inform Employees About the Change Effort Before It Commences. Be certain that they understand the reasons for the change program and what end result it is hoped will be achieved. Here it may be helpful to remember the uncomfortable fate of a person who attempted to institute change without such preconditioning (it is immaterial, of course, that the story may be apocryphal). As a foreman, this man was inordinately successful in initiating a major change in the actions and attitudes of his work crew, having carefully planned to tell them all the whys and wherefores, with ready answers to counter the ifs and buts. Later, as he advanced in position in his organization, this same person failed miserably when he had to effect a change where his foremen were concerned. Why? Unfortunately, he felt that because of their superior intelligence they would not need explanation and, therefore, he offered none. Intelligence, however, does not necessarily mean that intelligent people will more readily understand and accept change unassisted. Quite often, just the opposite is true—as intelligent employees use their advantage to rationalize reasons why change should not be effected.

Build a Trusting Work Climate. Mistrust in an organization arises when people have inadequate or incomplete information, when they are kept in the dark, when rumors disseminate false alarms. Under such circumstances, they tend to feel helpless; they suffer an uncomfortable psychological unbalance when they fear they cannot influence the situation in which they find themselves. It has been proven time and time again that people would rather have bad news than no news. Given the facts, they are more likely to feel they can cope with a new, even threatening situation than if they have no access to such information.

Use Problem-Solving Techniques. Identify the real causes of deep-seated negative attitudes; these rarely are generated by a single individual in a group. Be foresighted: It is almost always easier to influence people favorably toward the introduction of, for example, a data processing system before the installation is made than after a fait accompli is revealed. Make it possible for people to solve problems to their own satisfaction, and help them to do so; there is a much more positive reaction to change when those affected feel that they have been given all the facts and that they somehow were a part of the decision-making process.

Involve People in the Implementation of Change. In corporate situations particularly, allow employees to have a say in the way change is implemented. Take care, however, to distinguish between those who are merely critical in general and those who criticize constructively on the basis of information and experience. Often, the action skills essential to the implementation of well-thought-out change are only to be found among a silent minority of employees.

Ensure an Early Experience of Successful Change. In other words, do what must be done to facilitate rapid implementation of recommended and approved changes so as to build self-confidence among those affected. And, in the same vein, promptly celebrate and reward as appropriate when a change has been successfully accomplished; recognize those who have done a good job in bringing about the new situation—those who have helped rather than hindered.

Quickly Stabilize and Spread Successful Change. Perhaps the most critically overlooked and vital part of a change effort is that of timely assembly of a human support system dedicated to maintaining the new and different, the people in the organization who want to see it bear fruit. Another way to anchor beneficial change in one system is to make sure that it is appropriately effected in neighboring or allied systems.

Implementing Change

Lewin (1951) created what are now almost universally recognized as the three sequential phases of the change process: *unfreezing, moving,* and *refreezing.* We can identify many social forces that act to stabilize the behavior of individuals, and some of these forces are not unalterable natural phenomena, such as gravity. Lewin spoke of them as a "quasi-stationary equilibrium of forces." It is through change in the social forces acting on a person that his or her behavior is most apt to change—and the same principle applies at the group level.

The need for and the possibility of change first must be recognized by the persons involved, and the existing equilibrium must be made open to change, or unfrozen. Next, the social forces that are important and alterable must be identified and manipulated; this is the time-consuming part of any change process, largely because it results from painstaking diagnosis. But, when this step is successful, there will be evidence that the epicentric equilibrium has moved to a new position. This does not necessarily mean that such a change will be permanent. To forestall the new change reverting back to its original state, the altered social forces must be supported or stabilized. Often, this can only be accomplished by obtaining broad support from many persons or groups in the social system undergoing the change. Through this process of stabilization and generalization, the equilibrium is in a sense refrozen; the changes thus fixed are generally long lasting.

Lewin (1951) also introduced the familiar Force Field Analysis model that has long been helpful in understanding the pressures and counterpressures of the various impediments and inhibitions, supports and motivators that act to block or bring about change.

He looked on a level or phase of behavior within an institutional setting, not as a static habit or custom, but as a dynamic balance of forces working in opposite directions within the social-psychological space of the organization. He believed that we should think diagnostically about any change situation, in terms of the factors encouraging and facilitating change (driving forces) and the factors against change (restraining forces). These forces may originate inside the organization, or in the environment, or in the behavior of the change facilitators.

We can think of the present state of affairs in an organization as an equilibrium that is being maintained by a variety of factors that "keeps things the way they are." The change facilitators must assess the change potential and resistance and try to change the balance of forces so that there will be movement toward an improved state of affairs.

Change takes place when an imbalance occurs between the sum of restraining forces and the sum of driving forces. Such an imbalance unfreezes the pattern, and the level changes until the opposing forces are again brought into equilibrium. An imbalance may arise through a change in the magnitude of any force, a change in the direction of a force, or the addition of a new force.

Lewin pointed out that the effect of change will be maintained if the initial set of forces is unfrozen, initiates the change, and then refreezes at the new level. In many situations, however, the evidence of change is only temporary. Change in an organization is often followed by a regression toward the old pattern after the pressures affecting change are relaxed.

This model, however, does not reveal what must be done to keep a change frozen into its revised aspect. Here we get into change monitoring that usually involves a quiet barrage of interviewing and observing to learn how well the change is holding, supplemented by judicious data collection—and all tailored to determine whether the change is proceeding according to expectations and accomplishing its purposes. In addition, there is a need with every change to identify second- and third-order benefits, as well as negative consequences, and to see whether the change effort itself was sufficient to its purpose.

Effecting change means, of course, substituting for wishful contemplation the implementation of well-planned action. A written action plan for a change project is not a detailed presentation of how change will be accomplished; it does not show the context of each phase and step. But it does integrate related actions and jell the answers to pertinent preliminary questions: *Why* is the action needed? *What* is to be done? *Who* will do it? *When* will it be done and in what time frame? From *whence* will the required resources come? Moreover, careful consideration of these fundamentals tends to bring into sharp relief such things as limitations, deadlines, responsibility areas, and control mechanisms. We must remember, though, that Robert Burns's oft-quoted observation—"The best laid schemes o' mice and men, gang aft a-gley"—nowhere can be more applicable than in the business of effecting change. The foolish and naive among us tend to believe that change is accomplished in a snap of the finger by the chairman of the board or by the commander-in-chief, but the chairman and commander know differently. The grandest emperor has been powerless to bring about more than a temporary difference in the way things are done in the absence of fairly deep-rooted acceptance and commitment on the part of those affected. Lacking these two ingredients, most change efforts ordinarily are useless and result only in a continuation of the same. Acceptance of and commitment to change grow out of sufficient personal conviction that the new can be better than the old. There probably are as many ways to generate conviction in that genre as there are situations demanding change—and this is the essence of leadership in whatever mode; but basic to them all is the hidden concept that if the new is not better, there can be a return to the old. In effect, both the office manager and the platoon sergeant must couch their orders in an implied "try it once" attitude—except, and there always are exceptions, when there really is no alternative; and lacking an alternative to a given change (such as removing oneself from a house afire), neither acceptance nor commitment remain priority considerations—only the degree of success or failure.

For the sake of argument, therefore, let us assume acceptance and commitment. Neither is action itself. Neither is the trigger that causes unfreezing, moving, and refreezing. Take a look at the checklist in Table 4, in which the change manager, who is the top official of the organization or of that part of the organization in which change is to be effected, possesses the authority to investigate the need for and, if warranted, to implement change. Listed in the table are the various constituencies within the organization that can help the project manager in starting to make things different and better. But it does not end there. Implementing action to accomplish change can take a long time and suffer many a jolt.

One setback commonly encountered is the cost of more or less backsliding motivation. There can be four critical losses: (1) Competence deteriorates because of new roles, procedures, attitudes, and needed skills. (2) Relationships are warped due to revised organization structure and removed physical settings. (3) Power is dispersed as people enter different environments and old threads are parted. (4) Intrinsic rewards are devalued as a result of altered relative positions in the organization hierarchy or diminished opportunity for promotion that would have been there had not the table of organization been shifted. What is a manager to do? An action plan implemented in all or part of an organization benefits,

Table 4. Checklist for Taking Action.

Project Manager

Appoints a credible manager and gives him or her the authority, time, and resources to bring about the desired change.

Change Facilitators

Ensure that project manager has clout and the required skills.

Ensure that project manager has networks at all levels and in all parts of the organization.

Ensure that project manager has interpersonal and organization development skills to help, train, and coach those affected.

Ensure that project manager understands and can facilitate the phases of the change project.

Select and train the best people to carry out the action plan.

Motivate throughout the process people trying to change themselves.

Make available time and resources to those responsible for implementing the desired change.

Resource People

Give project manager external and internal consulting help in managing the change process.

Give project manager help in differentiating and integrating all change activities.

Give those responsible for action access to internal and external facilitators who collect data on change effect and who can recommend assistance needed by specialists.

Evaluation Team

Impartially measure the effect of actions taken against the purpose of the change.

Top Management

Maintain and demonstrate full support for the projected change and for the actions taken to achieve it.

first, from conscientiously tracing out all seven variables in the 7-S model (see Figure 4) and, second, from several sandbagging operations that do help hold in place the effected change. One might eclectically choose one or more of these:

Linking. This term is used to describe supportive actions undertaken throughout an organization to ensure that a planned change is not in conflict with ongoing, standing policies, practices, or procedures or to see that other inside or outside changes that are concurrently underway do not thwart or duplicate the planned change. This is essentially a matter of spreading the net of inquiry and information. In the ADM Strengthening Project, for example, we planned for an expected change in the World Bank's personnel appraisal and job classification systems—only to discover that a separate consultant group was working on job descriptions, causing duplication of effort.

Developing a Support System. Marrow (1974) describes five support systems used in a sizable change project. One such system leaned on the prior experience of others, calling upon top officials in other organizations to relate what had happened—good and bad—in similar change efforts. Another saw a team of behavioral scientists lead a one-week training seminar for the employees. A third marshalled the specialized skills of internal and external experts. The effectiveness of the change effort was measured and evaluated by a scientific task force, and responsibility for broad administration and guidance, as well as a direct tie to the training seminar, was assigned to a competent development and implementation team.

Enhancing the Competence of Those Involved. Here a change facilitator guides those affected by the change in adopting new behavior through training and coaching, a process that may require a reorientation of personal values, attitudes and beliefs, as well as behavior.

Avoiding Overload. Having too many concurrent change projects in the same organization is deadly to the momentum that might otherwise be gained by any one of them—and usually leads to a wholly predictable multiple breakdown. For example, imagine that in one organization, all at the same time, the accountants are installing a new budgeting method, planners are introducing a new corporate strategy, the personnel office is entering into attitude surveys and implementing new grading and appraisal systems, and the president is attempting to pull off a merger. This mish-mash is bound to blow a fuse.

Another safeguard against overloading (but one that offers no guarantees) is to establish alternative structures for the after-change process—that is, structures that are supplementary to the follow-through responsibilities of the "official" change management team. Beckhard and Harris (1977) proposed a choice of five such structures intended to involve others in an after-action survey of planning, implementation, and results. The simplest, of course, is line management responsibility—simple, but not always effective if a few soreheads remain. Another is to organize into a premonitory section representatives of the constituencies touched by the change, such as spokesmen for different departments, occupations, or self-interests (for example, a management/labor union task force). Consider, too, a suborganization of personnel specially trained as change agents or a matrix group of the natural, informal leaders in the organization who bring with them the confidence of a broad spectrum of the members. Also, superior in many ways—in some situations—is a study group charged with ongoing review and made up of a diagonal slice of employees that cuts across the levels and functions affected by the change.

Failure in Implementing Change

Crockett (1977), much to his credit, has enlightened us all by describing two unsuccessful, major change efforts at the U.S. Department of State in 1961 and again in 1967; on both occasions, he was responsible for the department's management. In lieu of a solid goal emplaced by either the President or the Secretary of State, he was told only that the Department of State must be made loyal and responsive to the President, that it must become more positive and proactive, and that it must assume a leadership position in the foreign service community. This was an exceptionally broad prescription, but Crockett felt he sufficiently understood the department, its problems, and their solutions because he had moved up through the ranks. His first diagnosis was devoted exclusively to interviews. On a globe-circling trip, he queried ambassadors, consuls, attachés, and foreign service officers. Principally, they readily complained of having no real authority in their assigned countries to coordinate and control the other American agencies, being ignorant of impending crises in other such agencies, and getting no back-up from Washington on critical, legitimate issues. Crockett identified a large number of bedrock issues and outlined 136 objectives to be accomplished. But an initial attempt to establish a leadership role for the Department of State among the overseas agencies of the United States government, which consisted of a directive from President Kennedy to set up a coordinating committee, fell quite flat in the bureaucratic swamp, and Kennedy found that he himself had to do the coordinating if there was to be any. Crockett, dismayed, decided that there must be something better than an authoritarian approach.

Nevertheless, the change effort continued. A step forward was made by developing a master plan for each country and bringing into existence an interagency policy-planning council. But before long the other agencies more or less openly characterized the concept as a useless paperwork operation—and used the master plan less and less. So Crockett was forced back to the drawing board. A policy-programming system was then worked out with the objective that each American ambassador would plan, fund, and measure the foreign affairs activities of all the United States agencies against the master plan for that country. Young, enthusiastic foreign service officers introduced the new idea at selected embassies. But both acceptance and commitment were lacking almost everywhere, and every decision required the intervention of the President or the Secretary of State. Attitudes remained unchanged; what seemed to change was illusionary, fleeting, and without faith. Thus, power and direction rapidly diminished, and with them the change effort. Crockett explains that rather than being due to lack of merit, both attempts foundered because of "the way they went about bringing them into being and trying to use them" (p. 111).

Failure, it has been said, more often than not results from pulling in one's horse as it is leaping. Crockett wondered if he himself was the one pulling in, particularly since attendance at a T-Group session gave him insights into how he was perceived by others. All managers and change agents have in their make-up a touch of supposedly negative characteristics; Crockett was not one to collapse under their weight.

Early in 1965, as top administrative manager, Crockett established an action program of organization development that was to concentrate on improving the effectiveness of the Department of State, increasing employee job satisfaction, and introducing a new style of management that would work with rather than against the environment. All of this called for using a machete in the bureaucratic jungle. First, there was planned a shift from a vertical to a flat hierarchy, removing the layering of authority that blocked both rising ideas and downward-directed policy. Six levels of supervision between Crockett and the operating managers were to be swept away, to be replaced by a concept of management by function, each functional manager reporting directly to the administrative manager. Decentralized functions would be centralized. Objectives, target dates, and resources were agreed upon and would be used to assess progress.

The change was announced to 450 subordinate managers by fiat. One hundred and twenty-five managerial positions evaporated; the incumbents in those that remained were to be trained to engage in participative planning. Each functional manager was helped to understand his or her role, responsibilities, and management style. A couple of hundred foreign service officers—some unhappily— were subjected to sensitivity training. Off-site, team-building exercises enabled open discussion of job-related problems and personal relationships, and this experience was sufficient to permit the managers to continue dealing with the cooperative aspects in their own realms, thus causing the healthy atmosphere of change first to cascade downward through the organization and then to solidify into refrozen attitudes and relationships. Managers themselves continued dealing with problems more openly and enhanced their work cohesiveness. External consultants helped the managers link their training to follow-up action and facilitated problem-solving meetings and group process feedback. Internal change agents were carefully selected and extensively trained; they became the benevolent eyes and ears of the managers with respect to whether the change was tracking or wheelspinning. The changes in structure and management style were so pervasive that adjustments had to be made in work flow patterns, decision-making loci, and paper processing. It is difficult to find serious fault with the procedure used. And yet all was in vain.

The planners were planning for a fait accompli, the teams were built only to carry out a dictum. Whatever value the change possessed—and it was considerable—was destined to be negated by the taint of overwhelming authoritarianism, only somewhat more for bureaucratic reasons than for misconception of the change process. The essential acceptance and commitment turned out to be superficial and transient *above* Crockett's level, and his successor was blithely permitted to restore the vertical hierarchy—by fiat. Perhaps some of the training proved worthwhile, and perhaps the Department of State is in some ways residually better off. But in the final analysis, the larger objective was not achieved in the time allowed.

After he had had an opportunity to put some time between himself and his experience managing the change process at the Department of State, Crockett emphasized these learnings:

- A major change in an organization absolutely must have the initial and unwavering support of top management.
- Restructuring an organization does not guarantee that people themselves will behave differently.
- Too much can be attempted too quickly.
- It is difficult to change a management style from authoritarian to participatory.
- Introducing a participatory approach to change in an authoritarian manner creates emotional disturbances and animosities that are slow to heal.
- The people affected by a change process must be involved in every phase; excessive reliance on diagnosis by external consultants of what needs to be done does not work.
- Subordinate managers must be helped to acquire a management style that supports the new norms and standards.

How Change Was Managed at the World Bank

Not all the future trends or guidelines cited previously were applicable to our change program, and we were indeed eclectic in our choice of those we applied. We did, however, follow the four fundamental steps of action planning, action implementation, control of the transition, and alternative back-up structures.

After the ten task forces and forty-three sub-task forces had been at work long enough—variously from six to ten months—it was decided by top management that all recommendations and action plans were to be submitted via the support group not later than the last day of December 1983. In Figure 6, we illustrate the series of progressive steps that successfully took the organization along a path from recommendations and action plans to review and acceptance to implementation. We believe this eight-stage change process is, generally speaking, a universally useful management guide.

The Essential Tool: Communication

Regardless of anything stated previously, we cannot too pointedly emphasize that—from the moment someone senses a need for change until long after a final crossing of the last "t" in a summary report of accomplishment—by far the most important element contributing to success is the art and act of communicating. Routine interoffice memoranda alone, however, are not sufficient unto this kind of communication. We refer also to generous, widely distributed feedback, to continuous written follow-up on action plans, to daily and weekly bulletins, in whatever form, for reading by managerial and nonmanagerial employees, to encouraging and commendatory memoranda from change process leaders, and, most helpful, to the publicized celebration of each successfully passed milestone by each level at which people participate in the change process. We refer to all these kinds of things being accomplished with complete openness—a "warts and all" candidness that deals as fairly with large and small failure as with large and small success, with oft-stated, unarguable consistency of objective and purpose and with a degree of timeliness that forestalls the nurturing of even miniscule doubt. This attitude, this spirit was admirably demonstrated at the World Bank in a memorandum from the change director to all participating employees after all the recommendations and action plans had been received by top management; it is quoted here in its entirety:

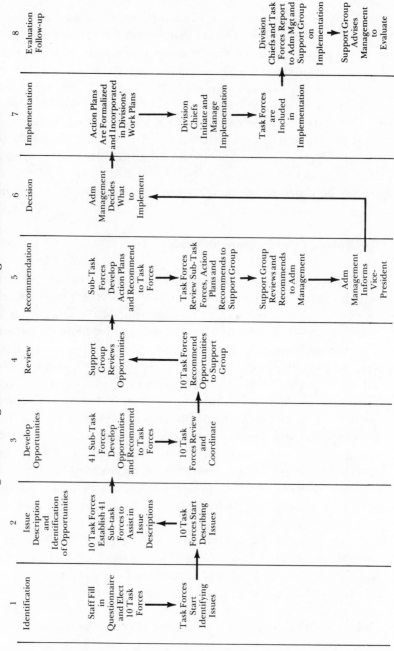

Figure 6. Management Guide for the Change Process in the World Bank.

Subject: Perpetuating the process and implementing the recommendations of the Strengthening Exercise in ADM.

1.   With the new year now before us, all task forces and, no doubt, ADM staff generally would like to know what steps are being considered to reinforce the excellent results achieved during the Strengthening Exercise. We are particularly indebted for the contribution made by our elected task force members. The net gain to each of us, and to the bank, is already being realized as a result of the greater understanding of our contributions to the bank goals and of heightened sensitivity to the aspirations, desires, and ideas of all of us.

2.   The momentum developed over the last eighteen months must be maintained, however. It is the role of departmental management and each and every staff member to remain fully committed to ensuring that the philosophy of participatory management and the recommendations developed, in some cases with considerable effort and pain, are implemented and made a continuing part of our operation.

3.   During the coming year, we will be implementing the broad range of recommendations which are now in the process of approval. I am pleased to report that several have already been carried out, but our greater concern rests with those slated for introduction after December 31, 1983.

4.   We do not intend to require that the divisions adopt any one particular process for ensuring implementation. We do, however, intend to use existing systems and procedures to monitor such implementation.

5.   These changes cannot be made overnight but will take some time to introduce fully. Over the next year, we will require some transitional mechanisms. I am expecting each division to continue to keep up its task force or set up some other participatory group to monitor implementation of its action plan and consider any new situations or opportunities which arise.

6.   It is also my belief that these committees should continue to be supported during the coming year. I have, therefore, arranged for the technical specialists of the support group to remain available to provide assistance with the implementa-

tion of action plans, as well as process consulting support if needed. The managing team will also remain on the scene in order to provide the essential contact between the task forces and the support group and to call meetings as necessary.

7. Without some specific action to institutionalize the highly desirable management philosophy which has started to emerge during the Strengthening Exercise, we would only be able to claim credit for a "one-shot" change.

8. We have already instituted this type of change by adopting as the department's overall mission statement the following twin goals, which stem directly from the Strengthening Exercise:

    (a) to provide support services to the bank that are appropriate, efficient, and economical; and

    (b) to maintain an environment which supports job satisfaction and individual growth of ADM staff.

    In pursuing these goals, we will need to formalize our approaches for examining the *appropriateness, efficiency,* and *economy* of services as a matter of course. In addition, we will have to broaden the *participation process* by adopting as a permanent management principle the practice of giving all levels of staff an appropriate decision-making role and by formalizing *career development* paths throughout the department.

9. It is my sincere wish and belief that by the end of this year a large degree of staff participation will exist at all levels in ADM. At the end of the year, we will review the situation to determine whether it is desirable to institutionalize some form of parallel system in which managers would participate voluntarily to carry on the spirit of the Strengthening Exercise but which would leave the responsibility to managers to carry on the department's business through the formal management chain.

10. In general, the approach by the ADM front office proves our commitment to following through with the Strengthening Exercise by not only monitoring that recommendations are implemented but also by institutionalizing many of the positive attributes which have developed as a result. Although introduction of many measures has already begun, I intend to

hasten the process by specifically assigning front office staff to take appropriate action. I will, of course, take full responsibility for ensuring the introduction and implementation of such measures.

11. There will be other communications from me on this subject. I look forward to keeping you fully informed as we move ahead with our action plans and the steps described above.

This memorandum shows continuing commitment by top management at the World Bank and signals the need for each employee to be equally committed. It makes clear that the desired changes will take time to materialize but that they all nevertheless will be closely monitored throughout. It expresses the intention to coordinate the changes achieved so far with the organization mission and stresses the five bedrock principles upon which each change was approved—appropriateness, efficiency, economy, participation, and career development.

An Example of an Action Plan Activated

Twelve months after action plans were submitted to the support group, the task forces made implementation progress reports. Skeptics, however, may wonder what the overall picture looked like a year after action plans were approved by top management. Figure 7 shows a recapitulation for the entire department at that time. Although 70 percent of the opportunities for improvement had been realized or were ongoing, the tabulation reveals the necessity to maintain a pressure on implementation across the board lest the divisional response become lost amidst day-to-day activities. Most of the deletions were justified because the recommendations had been overtaken by events internally—or because of changes in the external environment. Most of the actions that remained unimplemented were the responsibility of some other department of the World Bank and therefore were not under the control of the task forces or the ADM Department. And, as so often happens, changes begat changes; in some of the divisions that had a high percentage of actions completed, new task forces were finding newly revealed opportunities for improvement generated by the actions of their predecessor groups.

Figure 7. Opportunities Implemented as a Result of the ADM Strengthening Exercise.

Org. Unit	No. of Issues Identified	Submission Date	No. of Recom-mendations	No. of Sub-groups	Action Taken: Implemented 12 Months No.	Action Taken: Implemented 12 Months No.	Action Taken: Deleted	Action Taken: To be Implemented	Comments
A. Front Office	23	12/83	52	2	46	88	-	6	
B. Cartography	34	10/8/82	32	9	27	84		5 1/	1/ All these 5 are in progress but dependent on action to be taken outside Cartography.
C. Security	51	12/82	51	1	32	62	4	15	
D. Printing and Graphic	73	12/5/82	73	5	58	79	-	15	
E. Office Support Services Division (OSSD)	38	1/15/83	38	6	28	74	4	6 2/	2/ Several actions deleted because of changes in facility planning.
F. Communications Division	47	11/29/82	48	1	44	92	-	8	
G. Language Services Division (LSD)	9	12/10/82	16	8	11	60	-	5	
H. Records Management	37	12/23/82	111	3	37	33	7	67	
I. Procurement	8	1/21/83	24	3	15	63	-	9 3/	3/ All 9 will be implemented by 6/1/84.
J. Travel and Shipping	42	1/83	50	4	47	94	-	3	
Average Across Adm	362		495	42	345	72.9%	15 | 3%	139 28%	

Reflective Comments

Managing the change effort at the World Bank was fascinating and revealing. It tended to weaken drastically a number of organization development shibboleths and caused many of us to modify some of our own pridefully held convictions. There were counteracting forces at work. For example, among the resources offered to the task forces were the assistance of technical experts and process consultants; in a reversal of our anticipations, the former were lightly regarded and the latter generally were leaned on as crutch and mentor. We found that the sheer "adventure" of the change process was not as appealing as we thought it might be and that it was advisable—and productive—constantly to build in motivation. Despite the dangers of pushing too hard a delicate problem-solving process carried on by potentially cantankerous human beings, it was helpful to exercise the modest pressure of dated milestones and to meticulously review and revise at each stage so as to ensure that the change effort would be erected on firm ground. A more disciplined administration was needed than it was at first believed the managerial and nonmanagerial *employees* would require. Within the task forces themselves, there were conflicts and maladjustments in interrelationships that diplomatically had to be uncovered and resolved by an informal networking of process observers, internal and external consultants, and the project manager.

A major managerial concern for the overall change project—almost three years in duration and predictably subject to turnover in leadership—is whether the institution will stick with it. At this writing, the commitment is holding, but sooner or later motivation will have to be recharged and new people indoctrinated.

CHAPTER SIX

How to Evaluate Results

As we have seen, most planned organizational change follows a somewhat logical and fixed pattern: recognizing a problem, gathering data, making a diagnosis, planning a change action, and evaluating the results. Evaluation—which attempts to answer the haunting query, "Okay, what have we accomplished?"—usually will be derived from some data that, among other things, may be in the categories economic, human, financial, effectiveness, quality, marketing, productivity, or sales or any combination of these. It is not true, however, that managers or their consultants always complete these stages, particularly that of evaluation, with competence, thoroughness, or commitment. In an examination of some 160 change interventions, Porras and Berg (1978) found only 20 evaluation research studies that assessed organizational and work group change. In a survey of 76 consultants and clients, however, Bidwell and Lippitt (1971) found significant obstacles to collecting evaluative data (see Table 5). The important negative factors were lack of time and funds, inadequate frame of reference, and an inability to develop measurable objectives for which the change was attempted. While it is understandable that lack of time or funds might be hindering, it is interesting to observe how many respon-

Table 5. Obstacles to Evaluation Processes.

Obstacles	Number of Responses (N=52)*
1. Lack of time	20
2. Lack of a frame of reference (criteria)	15
3. Failure to determine expectations in measurable terms	14
4. Lack of money for research	12
5. Inability to convince management	9
6. Lack of effective research methods and tools	6
7. Need for adequate facilities and resources	3
8. Lack of cooperation between client and consultant	2
9. Magnitude of the research	2

* Twenty-three did not answer the questions and sixteen gave two or more responses.
Source: Bidwell and Lippitt, 1971, p. 11.

dents in this survey indicated their failure to establish a "frame of reference" against which to conduct evaluation research.

The Importance and Challenge of Evaluation

The dynamics of organization processes are complex and difficult to study. Can they be evaluated effectively? Yes, they can—if an appropriate evaluation approach is incorporated into the overall change plan. This means, inescapably, that evaluation and measurement plans must be a part of the initial planning phase that establishes the change process. But then planners of such processes need to ask themselves a few searching questions about evaluation: What should be evaluated? Why is it important? What will be gained from measuring results? How will the evaluation be accomplished, and who will do it? Who will collect the data and perform the analysis? What will be the time and dollar costs? What already existing data sources are available? Will the game be worth the effort? Who in particular should and will see the results? Why? Will the data obtained benefit the organization?

When push comes to shove in the board room, when the comptroller is poised to ask penetrating questions as to why, when the employees and junior managers are reaching their limit of tolerance for the sometimes disruptive oddities of behavioral science high jumps, a hard decision inevitably must be made as to whether to undertake the additional effort and expenditure of comprehensive evaluation of what has or has not been attained by an implemented change process. There are few hard and fast rules for guidance, but it is possible to run down a checklist of critical considerations: (1) How complex is the change? If the problem really is a number of problems or is extremely complex, it may not feasibly be possible to evaluate effectiveness. (2) How much time will be required to get the information in hand? (3) Is the question one of values or operations? If it is a matter of policy rather than measurable operations, evaluation may be attempting to nail down the ephemeral. (4) Might the costs outweigh the value of the data? (5) What will be the nonfinancial demands on the organization, such as extraordinary support, employee hours, public relations, and stress tolerance?

All of the above should not be interpreted as our painting evaluation as being overly difficult to achieve. On the contrary, evaluation—as does personality and the weather—exists without our lifting a finger; it is closer to the subjective end of the spectrum than to the scientific end, but it takes place irresistably before, during, and after any kind of change process. Similarly, of course, such gratuitous evaluation may be valueless and act as a purveyor of false signals, but if evaluation is directed and objective, it can be literally priceless. To be in any sense worthwhile, however, postprocess evaluation must be built into the initial planning and budget and wholeheartedly supported by top management from the first to the last day of the change process.

Experiences in Results Measurement

It is useful to relate an experience incurred by the United States Army in a change effort called Organization Effectiveness (OE), which involved behavioral science technology. OE was de-

signed in 1977 to deal with such ubiquitous problems as reenlist-
ment rates, morale, mobility, combat readiness, and officer/enlisted
relationships. Thus, OE was succinctly enough defined as "the
systematic military application of selected management and behavioral science skills and methods to improve how the total organization functions to accomplish assigned missions and increase
combat readiness. It is applicable to organization processes (including training in interpersonal skills) and when applied by a commander within an organization, it is tailored to the unique needs
of the organization and normally implemented with the assistance
of an Organizational Effectiveness Staff Officer (OESO)" [James
and Oliver, 1981, p. 6]. The OESOs who provided such assistance
were trained in a sixteen-week course given at Fort Ord, California.

James and Oliver (1981, p. 4), in their attempt to measure the
impact of the OE effort in the army, reported: "We were aware that
there was a dearth of objective data available on the outcomes of OE
operations. We also recognized that the sample of operations that
could be investigated might not be representative of OE operations
in general. To the extent that the sample was sufficiently representative, a set of generalizations could be made about the impact of
the OE program on the Army. *In order to assess the extent to which
the OE program achieved its operations objectives, we would need
to establish the degree to which the actual outcomes corresponded
to the objectives the Army had set out for the program.* Clearly, the
more representative the sample and the 'harder' the outcomes, the
more rigorous the assessment would be."

This points up the issue of whether evaluation should focus
on "soft" or "hard" measurement criteria. Soft criteria—attitudinal
and perceptual—usually are obtained from interviews, observations, and written survey instruments. Hard criteria—quantitative
gauges of job and system performance—usually are taken from
administrative records. As stated by Nicholas (1982, p. 531):
"Change in individual attitudes and behavior is a primary target of
Organizational Development, but these are 'intervening' variables,
and such changes are not necessarily followed by improvements in
group and organization performance. Even 'perceived' changes in
performance, based on soft measures, do not necessarily correspond
to 'actual' changes in performance based on hard measures."

Some change interventions seem to be more results oriented than others. Porras and Berg (1978) report an increase in the use of survey feedback and process consultation and a decrease in the use of the managerial grid developed by Blake and Mouton (1968), more laboratory training and variations in approach, with task focus enjoying greater popularity as process orientation slips, development of countering evidence to the once widely held notion that changed process causes changed outcome, frequent questioning of the effect of organization development on task-related behavior, and relatively little systematic proof of the efficacy of organization development. In the latter regard, Porras and Berg (1978) find that organization development in and of itself does not seem to make people happier or more satisfied; that it has an important effect only on individuals, rather than on organization process; and that such eccentricities as T-groups, encounter groups, and sensitivity training have resulted in the lowest percentage of reported successful change experiences.

There also can be stressed a valuable distinction among four kinds of data collection methodologies: *implementation research,* which focuses on finding solutions to specific organization problems; *assessment research,* which deals not only with outcome measurement but also with the process that produced it; *theory-building research,* which is oriented toward discovering fundamental relationships existing in a planned change; and *evaluative research,* which is concerned with the impress of a change intervention in terms of a total environment (Farchex, Amado, and Laurent, 1982). These two investigators highlight a new aspect of results measured by hard data—predicated on the most effective type of intervention. And, from a study of sixty-five published reports, Nicholas (1982) provides a categorization of interventions into three major groupings:

1. *Technostructural interventions:* The three elements involved here are job design and enlargement, job enrichment, and sociotechnical systems design. *Job design and enlargement* attempts to increase satisfaction and performance by consolidating work functions from a "horizontal slice" of the work unit so as to provide greater variety and a sense of the whole

task. *Job enrichment* is where work functions from a "vertical slice" of the work unit are brought together into a single job so as to provide greater task indentity and significance, employee autonomy, and feedback from the job. *Sociotechnical systems design* is directed at the fit between the technological configuration and the social structure of work units. This approach results in the rearrangement of relationships among roles or tasks or a sequence of activities that produce self-maintaining, semi-autonomous groups.

2. *Human process interventions:* Here we have survey feedback, team building, and structured laboratory training. *Survey feedback* is the systematic return of data to groups with the intent of encouraging discussion of problem areas, generating potential solutions, and stimulating motivation for change. *Team building* is a variation of laboratory training in which the emphasis is on improving team problem-solving ability and enhancing effectiveness in natural work settings. *Structured laboratory training* brings into play group experiences that concentrate on interpersonal behavior and the processing of issues and that enable specific learnings that can be transferred to the work setting.

3. *Multifaceted approaches:* These can be any combination of technostructural and human process interventions. They employ various techniques, usually implemented simultaneously; an example is the introduction at the same time of survey feedback, team building, and job enrichment.

It was interesting to observe that the multifaceted approach, when used at the World Bank, had longer-lasting effect in the change effort than the other approaches. This generously supported our theory of the superiority of the eclectic choice.

In a less extensive but still significant study, Steers (1975) asked seventeen changing organizations, "What criteria would you use to evaluate improved organization effectiveness?" The responses ranged from degree of adaptability/flexibility to downright survival, with all but the last more or less defying easy measurement. Although such a list of criteria is at best rather unhelpful, the researcher did derive a number of questions that place results evaluation in sharp perspective and that press upon managers and consultants a warning to avoid simplistic criteria:

- Is there any such thing as organization effectiveness?
- How valid and accurate are the assessment criteria?
- What time perspective is appropriate in making assessments?
- Are the assessment criteria related positively to each other?
- How widely can the criteria be applied?
- How do the criteria help us to understand the organization's dynamics?
- At what level should effectiveness be assessed?

Further, this study revealed that organization effectiveness should be viewed as a kaleidoscopic process, not as a fixed end state. This conclusion buttresses the eclectic approach we adopted at the World Bank and urges a grasp of as much up-to-date hard data as possible when measuring a fluid, dynamic situation that is a process.

In evaluative research, the practitioner and researcher initially must determine criteria by which to judge pluses and minuses resulting from an intervention—essentially asking the probing question, "Compared with what?" Peters and Waterman (1982, pp. 13-14) propound eight attributes, really eight variables, as the bedrock for reviewing performance by successful corporations—none of which is really new and few of which are conscientiously practiced. The eight attributes are: (1) A bias for action, for getting on with it; (2) Close to the customer; (3) Autonomy and entrepreneurship, where practical risk taking and innovation is encouraged; (4) Productivity through people; (5) Hands-on, value driven, where the basic philosophy of an organization has far more to do with its achievements than other factors; (6) Stick to the knitting, where the organization stays reasonably close to businesses they know; (7) Simple form, lean staff, where the organization structure is simple and top level staffs are lean; and (8) Simultaneous loose-tight properties, where activities that represent core values are centralized and autonomy through decentralization is arranged. Nevertheless, the act of developing means by which to measure success, so-so performance, or failure with respect to improvement in any one of these variables represents in itself the establishment of meaningful criteria. More elaborately and professionally, organization audits based on such criteria are being developed; one in particular shows great promise for the future. Stubbs (1982) has developed and tested a sixty-nine-item computer-scored audit of human resources. Here there is a cogent difference between this kind of examination, which asks people to evaluate their organization against a nonsubjective standard of excellence represented by core statements, and an attitude survey, which asks people for their subjective feelings. Rather than being a psychological test, an audit instrument is designed to gather descriptive and prescriptive hard feedback data with which to reinforce organization strengths and correct problems. It is, therefore, nearly ideal for use in evaluating the outcome of an intervention—especially so if employed before and after. In another attempt to identify and segment measurable criteria, Nicholas (1982) came up with four categories that are subject to hard valuation: *work force improvement* (turnover, absenteeism, grievances), *monetary measures* (costs, profits, sales), *productivity* (efficiency, effectiveness, quantity), and *quality* (of service, of product).

In a classic intervention, Lippitt and Swartz (1975) eclectically employed a variety of hard mensuration capabilities to perform a sophisticated review of post-effect safety performance at a large pulp paper mill—as compared with similar records of other like mills in the area. The data collection involved trend tracking and comparative analysis between pulp mills as related to accidents that affect efficiency of production. The purpose of this work was to test the hypotheses that: (1) Prior to the intervention, the number of accidents at Mill A was significantly higher than that of both Mill B and the industry average; and (2) After the intervention, the number of accidents at Mill A would decrease significantly. The null hypothesis was that the difference between the number of accidents at Mill A and in the rest of the industry in general would remain relatively constant, as evidenced by a Mann-Whitney U Test; the scores were combined and ranked in order of increasing size. The data were analyzed by comparing the pre-intervention data for Mill A and the Mill B industry average with the post-intervention data for Mill A and the Mill B industry average (see Table 6).

Table 6. Pre- and Post-Intervention Safety Measures at Two Pulp Paper Mills.

	MILL A Accident Frequency	Rank	MILL B Accident Frequency	Rank
	Safety Pre-Measure (1976)			
February	70.87	22	18.82	11
March	64.18	21	15.15	10
April	50.66	20	14.61	4
May	44.20	19	14.30	3
June	41.77	18	14.28	1
July	40.92	17	14.95	7
August	38.08	15	15.03	9
September	38.15	16	14.90	5
October	36.56	14	14.87	5
November	35.79	13	14.29	2
December	34.02	12	15.02	8
		$R_1=187$		$R_2=65$

Conclusions: The odds are one in a thousand that these results are due to chance. The accident rate was significantly higher for Mill A than for the Mill B industry average prior to the intervention.

	Safety Post-Measure (1977)			
February	30.30	17	15.45	10
March	10.07	8	12.65	9
April	9.39	7	15.55	11
May	8.94	6	16.08	13
June	7.28	3	15.96	12
July	7.76	4	17.05	14
August	8.03	5	17.54	15
September	6.82	1	18.13	16
October	7.19	2	----	--
		$R_1=53$		$R_2=100$

Conclusions: The odds are one in a hundred that these results are due to chance. The accident frequency is significantly lower for Mill A than for the Mill B industry average after the intervention.

Source: Lippitt and Swartz, 1975, p. 306.

In another situation with this same organization, a control group was used to measure the effectiveness of goal setting for production units. Some wood workers received special training and were permanently assigned, some received the training but not a permanent job, and some—the control group—were permanently hired but did not receive the extraordinary attention given the others. The results are shown in Figure 8. The time series also can be used without a control group, as for instance, measuring the effectiveness of a goal-setting intervention with respect to the productivity of truck drivers in a logging operation (see Figure 9).

In such results-type measurement, it is important to realize that other variables that are *not being measured* are acting on the change effect. When an organization change project, such as the ADM Strengthening Project or the U.S. Army Organization Effectiveness Program, involve multifaceted interventions, it is difficult to have specific means of measurement unless such criteria are established ahead of time—and evaluated before and after the intervention. Indicators of change effect with respect to work climate and issues can be obtained from an employee survey, where the data are graphically summarized in a form that can be used as a diagnostic instrument before and during the change process. By collecting data from the employees of the organization at the beginning of the change process and six months and eighteen months later, the graph can present attitude trends that are consistent with behavior observation and cost/profit related factors. Figure 10 illustrates an example of this taken from a company that has three major operating units. The graph shows the amounts of progress toward what management had established as ideal goals for the corporation in what were considered to be major areas.

Methods of Collecting Data for Evaluation

Five sources of evaluative information are most frequently used: *observation* and tallying individual, group, and/or systems behavior; *questionnaires* especially designed or in standard format that seek written responses concerning attitudes, viewpoints, opinions, and perceptions; *interviews* that involve face-to-face or telephone conversations that produce in-depth perceptions, concrete

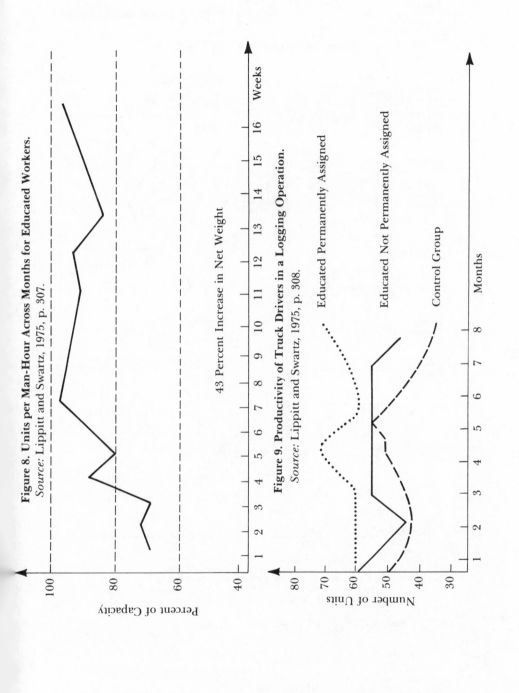

Figure 8. Units per Man-Hour Across Months for Educated Workers.
Source: Lippitt and Swartz, 1975, p. 307.

Figure 9. Productivity of Truck Drivers in a Logging Operation.
Source: Lippitt and Swartz, 1975, p. 308.

Figure 10. Organization Climate Profile.

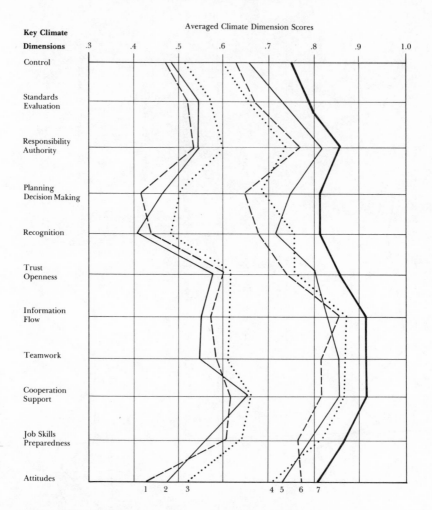

1. Nov. 1978 - Unit A Project Start Up   6. Nov. 1979 - Unit A Project Evaluation
2. Mar. 1979 - Unit B Project Start Up   5. Mar. 1980 - Unit B Project Evaluation
3. Nov. 1979 - Unit C Project Start Up   4. Nov. 1980 - Unit C Project Evaluation
7. Overall ideal as determined by management.

Source: Lippitt and Swartz, 1975, p. 309.

examples, expressed feelings, and ideas; *documentation* that includes extractions from current, archival, and/or special records; and *instruments* consisting primarily of feedback-collecting methodologies. Somewhat more to the point, however, the survey made by Bidwell and Lippitt (1971) revealed that at least a dozen methods are used in the inescapable data collection associated with change processes (see Table 7).

But the purpose of post-change research is not always for evaluation; other purposes include implementing action research, satisfying the organization's managers as to the usefulness of the change, improving the skill or performance of change agents, increasing business income, and changing organization relationships, among others. Implementing action research is prominently foremost among these purposes, but it is much more than a technology of evaluation, and it often occurs that "the roles of researcher and subject may change and reverse, the subjects becoming the researchers and the researchers engaging in action steps" (Lippitt, 1982, p. 307). If it is considered to be a process, a

Table 7. Methods Used for Evaluation.

	Number of Responses (N=64)*
Questionnaires	32
Interviews	16
Client Reports	14
Efficiency Reports	10
Discussions with client	9
Periodic testing	9
Inspections and visits	8
Consultant's ratings	8
Post evaluation immediately after consultation	7
Surveys of reactions to consultation	7
Surveys and operations audit	4
Follow-up testing (6 months to 1 year later)	1

* Eleven respondents did not list any methods, and thirteen listed four different methods.

Source: Bidwell and Lippitt, 1971, p. 5.

continuous series of occurrences, action research may be defined as the systematic collection of research data about an ongoing system relative to some objective, goal, or need of that system; feeding these data back into the system; taking actions by altering the selected variables within the system based both on the data and on hypotheses; and evaluating the results by collecting more data and repeating the cycle.

This definition of action research implies at least four major steps:

1.   *Data collection* may or may not be preceded by a tentative diagnosis of a problem area; it may utilize any of a variety of instruments for garnering task, environment, or attitude measurements.
2.   *Data feedback* should be given within a short time. It should be worthwhile to all participants and specific but without value judgments; it should be given in an open, supportive climate; and it should be relevant to desired goals.
3.   *Action planning* should be based on data collected and should be feasible within the organization's framework. All the people who will be involved in resulting actions should be participants in the planning.
4.   *Action* should have built-in standards by which to measure progress and results; it should lead naturally to more data collection and change if appropriate evaluation reveals a wrong direction taken.

Evaluating the ADM Strengthening Project

In light of the time, money, effort, and resources devoted to this change process, it is to be expected that the top managers of the World Bank would want to know what effect resulted from their extensive investment. After the process ended, the final analyses and recommendations were called in at the end of 1982, which was really too early to undertake a full evaluation. It was important, however, to obtain an *initial* reaction from a reasonable sample of the supervisors and employees of the ADM department, particularly from those who had participated in the task forces. The purpose of this early evaluation (Lippitt, 1983b) was to determine whatever improvement had occurred in ADM's efficiency, effectiveness, and working environment, to learn whether there was promise of anything at all being successfully changed, to estimate the usefulness of the activities employed in the change process, to see if the same approach might feasibly be used elsewhere in the World Bank, and, ultimately, to analyze how the collected data could be used to do more to improve ADM's services and working environment.

A model (see Figure 11) was developed for guidance in this preliminary attempt at evaluation. Although the model is self-explanatory, some explanation of the evaluation criteria is helpful. The *results measurement* was reduced to hard data concerning the direct effect of the project on such important factors as decreased costs, safety record, grievances, morale, absenteeism, efficiency, and client satisfaction. Behavioral observation reports, unavoidably soft data, were confined to changes in individuals and groups, such as voluntary reorganizations, simplified communications, and ability to implement problem solving. Other soft data included the observed and expressed *reactions* of participants in the change process with respect to their feelings, attitudes, and points of view, partially obtained through analysis of interviews and documents. Five sources of soft data were probed: management personnel of the ADM Department, World Bank clients served by the ADM Department, the consultants who were process observers, the employees who took part in the operations of the task forces, and, in summation, all employees of the ADM Department.

The soft data were collected for this purpose through (1) individual in-depth interviews, some as brief as half an hour, some as lengthy as an hour and a half; (2) documentation analysis, of which a main source was the division's reports of its progress toward defined goals; (3) group sessions, in which were included the task force chairpersons and support group leaders and from which were garnered comparative data and shared perspectives (see Table 8). A copy of the evaluation report was distributed to each ADM division. The conclusions reached from preliminary evaluation included both broad and narrow findings.

Figure 11. Evaluating the ADM Strengthening Project.

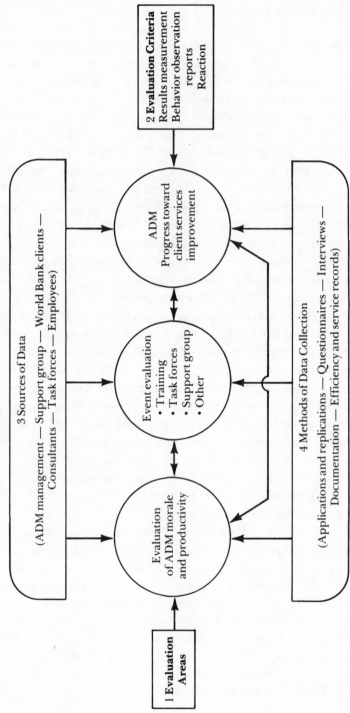

Source: Lippitt, 1983b, p. 21.

Table 8. Interview Schedule.

1. What role, if any, have you had in the ADM Strengthening Project?
2. What results, if any, have you seen at this time, of the ADM Strengthening Project? What were they?
3. What results of the Strengthening Project do you expect to see during 1983? In the long term?
4. What do you see as the major strengths and contributions to the World Bank of the ADM Strengthening Project?
5. What do you see as the major weaknesses and limitations of the ADM Strengthening Project?
6. How could the ADM Strengthening Project process, training, and administration be improved?
7. In what ways could the ADM Strengthening Project be applied to other sections of the World Bank? What changes in the process, if any, would be required?
8. What other comments would you make relative to the ADM Strengthening Project?

Source: Lippitt, 1983b.

General Findings of the Preliminary Evaluation

- The ADM Strengthening Project raised expectations of organizational change, improved planning, participative management style, better decision-making processes, and improved effectiveness and productivity. When expectations are raised, however, and management is perceived as not making an adequate response to those expectations, morale may be adversely affected. There was a great deal of skepticism about what would happen and even some cynicism. There was a need for prioritization—and all those involved needed to understand how and why the ordering took place.
- The effects of the project on production could not be ascertained, but a large number of new procedures were initiated that should lead to greater cost effectiveness.
- A need was expressed for top management to follow through on the project and not let it die of benign neglect; thus, most interviewees felt that the exercise was worthwhile, but some critics felt that it could be no more than a one-shot experience, completed and gone.

- Both employee morale and channels of communication were in general improved—and the ten divisions were seen as more client oriented.
- Employees seemed more committed to the ADM Department and to the World Bank but felt concerned about whether the "bureaucracy" would strangle the forward movement.
- During the course of implementing the change process, new and effective leadership emerged that might otherwise have gone unnoticed. But, apparently, this revelation was threatening to some managers and employees.
- Managers seemed to become more aware that in working with employees they must be sensitive to both task and process.
- All ADM Department employees felt that the change process had improved communications in and among divisions but that it still had a long way to go.
- Those interviewed felt that the ADM Department management team became more accessible and that a more open climate came into existence as a result of the Strengthening Project.
- A feeling exists that newly recommended innovations, operations, and organization will increase productivity and cost effectiveness.
- It was felt that the change process illustrated the virtues of participative management, but concern was generally prevalent that this was not the norm or the culture of the World Bank and that the present managers would not further the philosophy.
- There was little confidence in the permanence of any of the changes or in the idea that the expenditure of time and energy would show a "pay off" for the World Bank.
- There seemed to be an increased sense of unity among the employees and managers of the ADM Department.
- There was consensus that the change process proved that top management of the World Bank could "listen" to the ideas and concerns of its employees—and that this, in turn, helped the factors of recognition and involvement.
- The total structure and procedure of the ADM Strengthening Project was seen as appropriate, although some also saw it as cumbersome.

- It was believed that this process could be valuable to other parts of the World Bank—with appropriate revision and adaptation.

Specific Findings of the Preliminary Evaluation

- It became obvious that the division chiefs—and perhaps other levels of management—need supportive attention; some of them feel excluded, unappreciated.
- There seemed to be a general perception that the periodic progress reports were intended to punish managers for slippage rather than serving as an aid in improving management planning.
- More division chiefs are now holding regular, participative staff meetings, but there still is need for improvement in this respect.
- The regularly published newsletter was seen as valuable to employee communication and morale.
- There has been a reduction in paperwork and duplication.
- Some persons stated that their leadership in the change process may have caused them harm with their noninvolved division chiefs.
- It seemed that a few members of the front office of the ADM Department had not supported the change process sufficiently.
- The change process occurred at a time of many other changes at the World Bank, and it was therefore difficult for some employees to assimilate all the changes simultaneously.

Broadly speaking, this early evaluative data clearly indicated that for the time being there had been noticeable improvement in the ADM Department's internal and external communications and in its internal personnel relationships—resulting in an apparent increase in participation/collaboration and in planning/productivity. The managers observed personal growth on the part of many of the employees and perhaps a corresponding enhancement of morale. A tangible manifestation of problem solving had been developed and, doubtlessly collateral, a sense of departmental unity. Whether these benefits remain in place must be determined by more searching evaluations twelve months and eighteen months after the planned change process was considered completed.

Stepping back a few paces so as to obtain a more inclusive perspective, it can be seen that this change process left the ADM Department in a stage of transition. Everyone was willing to give the situation a chance to work itself out for the good of all, but throughout the World Bank there was inculcated a charitable "wait and see" attitude. There is a philosophical aspect to the implementation of a change process in one department of a large organization. A person standing on the edge of the Grand Canyon was overheard to say, "Something happened here! It is obvious that this enormous chasm is not the result of someone dragging a stick in the sand." Even the preliminary evaluation of what was accomplished by this change process indicated that "something happened here" and that it had happened by design. More important, the data indicated that things were continuing to happen that solidified the practice of participative management. After so much to-do over so long a time, it is easy to understand why an evaluation was somewhat impatiently sought, regardless of the fact that such a reading probably was premature. But there was another thought behind such an evaluation, namely that it would have almost immediate utility:

- for the ADM Department in sharing with the top World Bank managers the results of this project
- for top management in long-range development planning at the World Bank
- for personnel and training managers in evaluating the strengths, weaknesses, and development needs of the World Bank as an organization and its role in human resource development and utilization
- for personnel and training managers in interpreting the functions of their units within the World Bank
- for the ADM Department in clarifying and assessing its identity and function within the World Bank
- for the ADM Department in establishing professional development objectives for its employees
- for the ADM Department in planning objectives for client relationships and for services to the World Bank
- as a resource for professional communication with colleagues in the ADM Department

- as a comparative basis for Phase II of the evaluation process
- as a document to share in part or totally with those who were interviewed in this evaluation process
- in identifying steps to be taken to ensure follow-up on the recommendations made by the ADM Department

Despite these useful information gains, there were some crippling faults in this preliminary evaluation of the ADM Strengthening Project. The evaluation was not planned at the beginning of the project, with the result that both pre- and post-process data could not be collected. While some criteria for improvement were established, most of the measurable hard data came out of action recommendations made by the task forces, with subsequent results scheduled for measurement in November 1984 during the second evaluation phase. This evaluation report was made only six months after the completion of a year-long change process, too soon to measure results in areas such as restructuring, job performance, productivity, quality control, and so forth.

What, in terms of positive action taken as a result of the preliminary evaluation, did the upper eschelon of management at the World Bank think of the results of the ADM Strengthening Project? Its initial reaction, late in 1983, was to promote the project manager to the position of director of the Administrative Department. This new director could well have rested on his laurels, but he did not. He promptly reactivated the support group, requested each division to establish a task force to monitor progress toward the goals highlighted by the change process, initiated training assessments, recalled former consultants, developed new work standards, reorganized two units, and—certainly not without significance—changed the incumbents in a number of critical managerial positions.

Reflective Comments

The major learning from the preliminary measurement of results has been that evaluation should be planned at the moment of initiation of a change process. It cannot be an afterthought. In addition, it is important to develop evaluation criteria so that *both* hard and soft data are collectable and collected. Our principal concern about the preliminary evaluation was that it was implemented too early to really obtain measurable results. The Phase II evaluation scheduled for Fall 1984 will be able to measure the actual number of changes implemented by each of the ten divisions and to provide more specific data about the progress and success of the project.

CHAPTER SEVEN

Effective Change: Lessons from Experience

The turbulence faced today by organizations is caused as much by the increased complexity of their technological functions as by revolutions in our contemporary society. In addition, predictable strains are being exerted on organizations by more dynamic interrelations and increased interdependence among government, industry, communities, and education. These multiple forces must be met with a process of organization renewal, adaptation, and planned change. As stated by Gardner (1969, p. 40): "The true task is to design a society (and institutions) capable of continuous change, renewal, and responsiveness. We can less and less afford to limit ourselves to routine repair of breakdowns in our institutions. Unless we are willing to see a final confrontation between institutions that refuse to change and critics bent on destruction, we had better get on with the business of redesigning our society."

Standards for Organizational Change

Recognizing that organizational change and development is a requirement is not the same as being able to initiate and succeed with such a process. The challenge for management today is precisely the ability to implement the change process. And yet what have professionals, practitioners, and researchers in the field learned that helps management meet such a challenge? In the past half century, many models of organization have evolved from management philosophies and are now used to guide management practice. One attempt to sort out these models was undertaken by Davis (1968), who from the standpoint of historical chronology, separates the *autocratic, custodial, supportive,* and *collegial* models. He feels that early on the autocratic model tended to predominate; in the 1930s and 1940s it yielded ground to the custodial or paternalistic, and in the 1960s and 1970s the supportive model gained approval and reached ascendency in a number of organizations. Davis (1968) also points out that in the 1980s some high-tech and advanced organizations will be experimenting with the collegial model. The point is that each successive model has served a higher order of needs and complexity than the last and is more responsive to the changed nature of man and society. The effort at the World Bank pushed toward the collegial model.

In later research, Vaill (1982) examined high-performing systems, looking for definition of excellence in organization functioning. He concluded that one or more of these criteria of organizations prevail:

- They are performing excellently against a known external standard.
- They are performing excellently against what is assumed to be their potential level of performance.
- They are performing excellently in relation to where they were at some earlier time (developmental criterion).
- They are judged by informed observers to be doing substantially better qualitatively than other comparable systems.
- They are doing whatever they do with significantly fewer resources than it is assumed are needed.
- They are perceived as examplars of the way to do whatever they do, and this becomes a source of ideas and inspiration for others (style criterion).
- They are perceived to fulfill at a high level the ideals for the culture within which they exist—that is, they have nobility.

- They are the only organization that has been able to do what they do at all, even though it might seem that what they do is not that difficult or mysterious a thing.

In their deliberations and differences, the participants in the task forces at the World Bank knowingly or unknowingly used for various comparisons all of these concepts of excellence.

There is reactive, proactive, and interactive planning for change (Ackoff, Finnel, and Gharajedaghi, 1984). *Reactive* is from the bottom up and tactically oriented, usually carried out independently in only a part of an organization. *Proactive* is from the top down and strategically oriented. *Interactive* consists of designing, developing, and selecting a desired future, and here the principles of participation, continuity, and holism are strongly evident. All three modes of planning were to one degree or another involved in the change process at the World Bank. There was considerable participation at all levels and much attention was given to the purpose of the Administrative Department, but the change process was not holistic in terms of organization-wide coordination and integration. This is understandable in terms of resources and unfortunate in terms of what might have been accomplished on a larger scale. As explained by Ackoff, Finnel, and Gharajedaghi (1984, p. 118): "When the principles of coordination and integration are combined the holistic principle is obtained; every part of an organization at every level should plan simultaneously and interdependently. The concept of all-over-at-once planning differs significantly from both reactive bottom-up and preactive top-down planning."

Learnings from Others' Change Experiences

In this respect, it might be appropriate to start with a learning from Harrison (1970, p. 201): "First, to intervene at a level no deeper than that required to produce enduring solutions to the problems at hand; and second, to intervene at a level no deeper than that at which the energy and resources of the client can be committed to problem solving and to change." In other words, meet the needs of the organization at a level at which it can and will use and apply the help. Vaill (1973, p. 25) notes another aspect of the change process when he says: "The social sciences, organization development has taught us, are interventionist even when they are not trying to be. One cannot study a human system without changing it, and since no two human systems are identical, the interventions are irreversible: we cannot know what the system would have been like or what would have been discovered there had the investigators chosen to collect data from different people than they did, or on different issues than they did, or with different methods than they did."

The theories that lie behind such approaches as Beckhard's (1967) confrontation meeting, Weisbord's (1978) helpful mechanism, Blake and Mouton's (1968) managerial grid, and many others became the intervention itself according to Foltz, Harvey, and McLaughlin (1975). Early in the history of attempts to initiate organization change, the efforts were atomistic, and those who labored in the field soon learned the interdependence of factors, forces, levels, and systems that simply had to be considered. Vaill (1973, p. 25) described this situation well:

> Another way to say what organization development has learned is that it has been forced to rethink what the salient elements of the client system are without unconsciously assuming that the only thing of interest there is the people. In order to introduce change effectively, one has to be interested in the whole system—the people and all the other things that are there. In order to understand such situations, organization development has needed to learn to talk about all the elements of the situation at about the same level of abstraction, rather than the people at a low level and everything else at a high level. This has been a painful learning for organization development. All through the 1960s organization development tried to ignore technology and the business realities of the organization and the environment it existed in. But in the last ten years organization development has become more and more comfortable with the fact that

the whole system must be the object of change, and the *whole* system is a stew of people and things and factors, not a homogeneous and regular phenomenon at all.

Success and failure in organizational change—the essential learnings from the empirical experience—have in a way identified certain emerging criteria:

1. Is the change effort based on an articulated value system in which the purposes of the organization are clearly related to those it serves? Management should express the values it espouses and manifests. When this is done satisfactorily, the change effort then can undertake, with competent awareness, the reinforcement of the attitudes, skills, and knowledge that contribute to the organization's culture, and it will be in a position to monitor the degree and manner in which new values are inculcated or old values modified.

2. Does the change effort take into account the essential needs of the organization in its present state? An organization develops differing needs, depending upon its stage of growth. A small organization trying to establish itself may require a few dynamic and autonomous executives who behave semi-autocratically in defined areas of responsibility. A large organization with multinational offices has a need for executives who can coordinate and communicate through others. The well-established organization with years of success behind it may well want its executives to concentrate on community and other external relations that can contribute to larger service goals. Such differences should be continually assessed in establishing and executing the objectives of organization development projects; to be operating in the wrong area of need can indeed be frustrating.

3. Is the change effort process based on the realities of future change? Survival of tomorrow's organization, as well as achievement of excellence in a rapidly shifting industrial, governmental, international complex demands that leaders today be quite adaptive and that the lower-eschelon managers

and all employees under their influence and guidance be creative, tolerant of ambiguity, and capable of timely self-adjustment. A conceptual vision and a practical awareness of the probable nature of the organization's near and distant future should be captured and held through all its nuances of change by those who are involved in a change process.

4. Is the change effort based on well-defined organization objectives and plans? Management by objectives and strategic planning have been thoroughly propounded in management literature during the past twenty years. Plans for a change process should translate overall goals into individual and work unit objectives, because success in human endeavor inevitably is related to meaningful achievement of personal and group goals. Individuals and groups in a change process need to know and understand the goals toward which they are striving or being pushed and to be familiar with the criteria to be used in evaluating desirable change in their performance.

5. Is the change project predicated on examples of successful and unsuccessful criteria of effective performance? Management thinking frequently is curtailed by the reluctance of those on whom they rely for planned change to define effective performance, both positive and negative. There is no uniform standard. The kind of managerial excellence required in a large steel company may be different from that most desired in a large government agency. Skills of entrepreneurship that are advantageous to a small clothing company may vary remarkably from those that are essential in a small research and development firm. A well-conceived change project should be based on thorough information regarding the characteristics and capabilities needed at each managerial and nonmanagerial position in that particular organization.

6. Is the change project designed to modify or reinforce individual attitudes as well as to develop applicable skills and knowledge? If a change project contributes only the acquisition of new knowledge, there may be no substantive change in performance—because so limited a contribution provides no foundation for skill development and attitude reformation

in the actual practice of new behavioral patterns. The most meaningful aspect of personal change is the self-examination and alteration of beliefs, values, and shared hopes for the organization by those who work within it.

7. Is the change project in all respects specifically designed for the organization to be effected? There probably never will be such a thing as a universally applicable organizational change process (and, therefore, the great advantage of the eclectic choice). Canned or packaged efforts that emphasize one skill or another may be of questionable benefit unless it is obvious that such skills can be woven appropriately into the fabric of a larger, well-rounded process that considers multiple organization needs and that precisely fit that organization—and the individuals and groups within it.

8. Is the change project to be professionally planned, created, and implemented? Any process for improving the functioning of an organization should make use of all that is known about learning processes and theory, educational methods, group and organization behavior, organization theory, and similar fields of knowledge. Whether guidance comes from within or without the organization, professional planning, designing, and implementation is vital; more damage than good can be wreaked in this complex field by the inexperienced and unknowledgeable. It is our conviction that the responsibility for change should be in the hands of line management; the specialized help these line managers may want or need is best provided by professionals working as a team both internally and externally.

9. Is the change project supported by leadership practices and an open systems climate within the organization? A productive planned change almost invariably means that something different will be effected in individual and organization practices. Reinforcement and follow-up are essential to freezing and maintaining learning at new, higher levels. Two major factors must be present, however: the behavior of senior executives should manifest support for and belief in the change project so as to establish a climate in which achievement is possible, and desired change in performance should

be equitably rewarded by promotion or increase in pay or by some other concrete indication that a goal has been reached and that such achievement is appreciated and acknowledged.

10. Does the change project provide for evaluation in terms of long-range organization goals? The predictable effect of a change process, as well as its immediate results, should be carefully studied by the leaders of an organization as its needs change—or appear to change. A "happiness ratio" can and usually is easily obtained from the comments and testimonials of individuals who have participated in or are affected by a particular aspect of such a process, but available research methodology for assessment at a deeper level should be used to ascertain the real results affecting organization, group, or individual goals. There is a danger that without the guidance of such deeper analysis, a change project may prove to be culturally superficial rather than meaningful with respect to change toward predetermined standards of excellence. More- over—to repeat—the means of evaluating short- and long- range achievement should be devised in advance, before any plan for change is implemented. Objectives then found not to be compatible with achievement measurement undoubtedly also will be found to be not worth the expense and effort necessary to gain them.

From now on, those who assume responsibility for organi- zation improvement will be judged by their overall contribution to the entire system. The present-day approach to organizational change evades the purely mechanistic process, the directed develop- ment of managerial skills, and the "its only a human relations activity" syndrome. A properly planned and implemented change project is a systems-oriented approach utilizing human, financial, and technological resources; it must be interdisciplinary in scope and thought.

Learnings from the World Bank Project

The change effort within the Administrative Department provided a cornucopia of valuable experience to those who were involved as planners, consultants, observers, and process leaders. The most important learnings were in these categories:

- Employee participation and involvement
- Management support and involvement
- Use of training to support change
- Importance of an information system
- Need to utilize resources effectively
- Organization climate, values, and culture

For each of these broad categories, we cite the learning we experienced and the generalized applications that are implied:

Employee Participation and Involvement

Learning	*Application*
A participative change process can identify needs, but it may also create more expectations than can be met by management.	In order to clarify and limit expectations, top management should respond to concerns and needs proportionately in four areas: the good ideas that should be implemented; those good ideas that require too much time, effort, or money to implement; those ideas that are inappropriate; and lastly, those ideas that for any reason must be vetoed.
Allowing employees to elect task force members to identify change needs created more trust in management.	An organizational change effort needs to involve employees at the earliest stages of planning for change.
Employee involvement creates more and newer ideas for change than can be generated by management, staff experts, or outside consultants.	Call upon employees to contribute ideas about improving the quality and quantity of work— because they are closer to the actual implementation of the expectations of management.

Employees are experts in their own area of specialization and should be involved and consulted.

Take advantage of those workers—whether technical, professional, or hourly—who are able to see the simplification and complexity of their work more thoroughly than any manual, consultant, or survey; their data are invaluable in examining work enlargement, enrichment, reorganization, or change.

Management Support and Involvement

Learning	*Application*
Support of top management is critical to the success of any change effort.	Start the planning for a change effort as close to the top of the organization as possible.
Direct involvement of nonmanagerial employees may threaten the security and status of middle managers.	In a change process, secure the involvement and commitment of *all* levels of management.
Overdependency on one manager as project leader may lead to other members of the management team not fulfilling important responsibilities.	Roles of all managers involved in the change process should be negotiated, articulated, assigned, and publicized.
Top management must coordinate with a change project coordinating group (at the World Bank, the support group) so that task force recommendations may be channeled into vital action areas.	A change process must be viewed as an integral part of the day-to-day functioning of the organization, not as a "once only" stimulus or effort.

Use of Training to Support Change

Learning	*Application*
Persons serving as task force chairpersons or members need to be trained in their roles and responsibilities.	Ensure competence in such functional positions by making their training in new role behavior an essential part of the change process.
The skills of being a process observer are new to many persons, whether employees, internal or external consultants, or managers.	Optimize the effectiveness of this important function in the change process by taking the time and devoting the effort to train well those who are to fill this role.
Specialized internal and external resource specialists must be adequately trained so as both to direct their contributions and to contain their activities.	Those technical persons selected to assist the problem solvers must not be allowed to take over the problem; rather, they should be made to see their role as advisor or consultant to the task force members.

Importance of an Information System

Learning	*Application*
At the initiation of the change project, the development of a model and common language proved to be helpful.	To help the people involved in a change process, there should be a minimum of professional "gobbledygook"; but, when necessary, everyone should be able to share a common language for describing elements of the process, personnel, and procedures.

The creation of a source or reference book that gives all the participants a basic understanding of the purposes and procedures of the change process proved to be invaluable; the ADM Strengthening Project *Survival Kit* served as a bible for one and all.

Provide a notebook or guide book to all participants in the change process not only to help them understand the goals to be attained but also to establish the reality of the project.

Follow-through was increased when attainable goals were set, steps were identified, and dates for accomplishment were agreed upon and written down.

Establish quickly in any change process the specific information of what is to be done, how it is to be done, and when it is to be done.

When data, suggestions, and recommendations are submitted to a coordinating group, it is essential that feedback be shared with the originating group.

The flow of information must be a two-way street; people want to know what is going on so that they can remain involved, informed, and ready to respond to the next phase of the change process.

Need to Utilize Resources Effectively

Learning

Application

A support system for the project leader is an essential part of a change project; without such support, a change effort is likely to become too individualized, focused on one person's drive and charisma.

Ensure actual and moral support for the project leader by top management, middle management, supervisors, and his or her peers.

Specialist units within the organization, such as personnel, organization planning, and research and development, can block the change effort unknowingly.

Such specialists must not be allowed to take over the change process; they must be seen and must view themselves as valued resources, needed by the line organization and members of the task forces.

Process observers provided an essential function in keeping the change process on the track; they were invaluable to the task force leaders in the World Bank change process.

The function and role of process observers should be seen by all as vital to any change effort—particularly when several groups (task forces, in this instance) are participating.

In the World Bank effort, the middle managers sometimes felt left out of the process.

Line management at all levels needs to support not only the change process but also the actions of the middle managers. Success or failure depends on line managers at all levels implementing approved improvements in their areas of influence; therefore, all managers should be informed, involved, challenged, and appropriately encouraged to do their best to make the change process work.

Use of internal and external consultants is helpful in a change process, but these helpers must be controlled, integrated, and coordinated.

In order to ensure cooperation and progress toward common goals, internal and external consultants and technical advisers should be enlisted on the same team and made subject to direction of a central authority.

Organization Climate, Values, and Culture

Learning	*Application*
A planned change will be affected by unplanned changes; in the fifteen months duration of the ADM Strengthening Project, twenty-five other simultaneous change efforts included a climate survey, the physical relocation of a major office complex, a new appraisal plan, new employee pay scales, and a cutback in budget.	In planning a change effort, the planners should try to foresee or learn about all other forthcoming events, sensing the existing and future realities that will affect the organization, and, when feasible, attempt to integrate these parallel change projects into the overall picture.
When planning organizational change, it is desirable to build in the evaluation plan at the beginning; if this is not done, it is difficult to establish post-event criteria for effective measurement.	Management and change process planners should anticipate hard measures of the results of the change effort.
Open communications for identifying problems must be encouraged and rewarded, or employees will feel threatened by supervisors who believe them to be troublemakers, gripers, and uncooperative workers.	Change effort planners must ensure stated and unstated reward systems relative to openness and trust; provision must be made for rewarding, celebrating, and acknowledging creativity, new ideas, and innovation.
A change effort will take time, use up resources, and cost money—all of which brings up the question: Is the process worth the effort?	The plans for a change effort should try to project a quid pro quo between the time and money to be spent and the hoped-for results in such factors as less personnel turnover, fewer accidents, and increased productivity.

If a change process involves a value, such as participative management, that differs widely from the existing culture of the organization, change will be difficult to achieve; the process must be representative of the organization's culture—or an acknowledged attempt to confront that culture.

Preliminary tests should be made to determine whether the desired new values conform to the concepts of management, employees, and the policy makers.

The foregoing has dealt with the learnings, means, and difficulties of organization transition at the World Bank. Of the fact that change has taken place there can be little doubt; that change ensues is a certainty. If one likens the Administrative Services Department at the World Bank to a ship afloat on the sea, which is her environment, then the poetic, intriguing words of Arthur Hugh Clough (1819-1861) have a considerable depth of meaning:

> Where lies the land to which the ship would go?
> Far, far ahead, is all her seamen know.
> And where the land she travels from? Away,
> Far, far behind, is all that they can say.*

This much we know: the ship is in fine condition, the men and women of her crew are happy, she is making good progress toward lasting improvements; but just where she will finally tie up is not exactly known—more because at best her change effort charts and instruments lack finite accuracy than because her skipper is an unwise navigator. He has set ashore his pilots—the advisers, assistants, and consultants—lest he and his crew become too dependent on them, and he trims his sails carefully so as to ensure a

---

*Source: Arthur Hugh Clough, "Where Lies the Land." *Oxford Dictionary of Quotations*. London: Oxford University Press, 1953.

timely and smooth passage. There is every reason to anticipate a successful voyage.

We believe you may find interesting this concluding report on the ADM Strengthening Project:

Administrative Services Department Strengthening Exercise
Final Report

Background

1. The July 20, 1981, report by the Organization Planning Department (OPD) entitled *Diagnostic Review of the Administrative Services Department Front Office Organizational Structure* recommended (in addition to the restructuring of the department with two assistant directors, as was done) "an in-depth and thorough review of the Administrative Services Department (ADM) *from within* under the direction of the deputy, as well as the development and implementation of new departmental planning and control systems." Following discussions with OPD and the Personnel Management Department (PMD), a strategy for strengthening ADM was further developed at a Harvard Business School course on managing organizational effectiveness and then refined with input from a support group[1] created to design, monitor, and provide assistance in what became known as the ADM Strengthening Exercise.

2. The ADM Strengthening Exercise was launched with your sponsorship in October 1981 at a meeting of all ADM supervisors and line managers, and the various task forces throughout the department completed their action plans and sub-

[1]Original members of the support group were R. E. Barry, ADM; Gavin Duncan, Coverdale consultant; Cathrine Fox, PMD; Petter Langseth, PMD/OPD; Katharine Lawrie, PMD; Gordon Lippitt, George Washington University; Ralph McConnell, ADM; Jack Mossop, PMD; Sam Niedzviecki, OPD; Irene Normandin, ADM; Gulshan Sachdeva, ADM; and Clifton Senf, ADM. Others assisted as the exercise progressed. Each person knows better than I how much he or she contributed. Each person's contribution, large or small, was important to the success of the exercise.

mitted them to you for your comments and approval early in 1983. I believe it is appropriate at this time to submit a final report on that original change effort in this department to set the stage for the future.

3.   In preparation for this report, the support group met with representatives of the task force of each division and of the Director's Office. At each of these meetings the following questions were asked:

- Are there any outstanding issues from your action plan?
- Are new issues being handled through the strenthening exercise mechanism?
- Do we have evidence of improved client satisfaction (such as more efficient, effective, economic, and appropriate services)?
- What have been the barriers to progress?
- What can the support group and Director's Office do to help?

4.   While a reading of these detailed discussions will reveal that there were different areas of concern in each task force, in the paragraphs that follow I have extracted my perception of the common denominators.

Outstanding Issues from Action Plan

5.   The number of outstanding issues varied widely from one division to another. [As shown in Figure 7 (see Chapter Five),] out of the 495 recommendations that were formally submitted, 345 or 70 percent had been implemented twelve months later. In five of the divisions, more than 80 percent of the actions had been implemented. Only 3 percent of the recommended actions were deleted, and in most cases these were deleted because changes in the external environment made them redundant. Of the actions still to be implemented, the majority were out of the control of the task force and/or divisional management.

Are New Issues Being Handled Through the Strengthening Exercise Mechanism?

6. New task forces have been elected to replace the original task forces in five of the divisions. In the ADM Director's Office and three of the divisions, meetings of the work unit as a whole are called to follow up on the original actions of the task forces and to deal with new issues. In one division, the implementation of the recommendations and the new issues are dealt with through meetings at the level of the work unit and communication through the management chain. Opinion is divided amongst staff in the department as to whether the task force mechanism should remain in place. Those who wish to keep it feel that there is still a need to be able to communicate directly with senior department managers. Those who no longer see the need appear to be relatively satisfied that procedures existing within their division allow them sufficient opportunity to express their concern.

Do We Have Evidence of Improved Client Satisfaction?

7. There was a general feeling that clients are more satisfied with services in ADM now than they were three years ago. In several cases, this can be seen in the results of survey questionnaires. Most divisions, however, express the reservation that there had been other changes taking place at the same time as the strengthening exercise, so that they were reluctant to attribute all of the improved client satisfaction directly to the results of the ADM Strengthening Exercise. Almost without exception, there was a feeling that the strengthening exercise had created improved communication within the work unit, and this was seen to be a positive contribution.

What Have Been the Barriers to Progress?

8. Most task forces commented that the principle barrier to progress was a lack of time to work on the ADM Strengthening Exercise because of competing demands to continue providing service. Nevertheless, as we know from our time records, those staff who were actively involved did contribute

a significant portion of their time, even if it required working overtime or spending some of their personal time on the exercise. There was a feeling among a number of task force members that the lack of support from some line managers up to the top of the department had been an impediment to change.

What Can the Support Group and
ADM Director's Office Do to Help?

9.   The majority feeling seemed to be that the support group should remain in place to provide encouragement and guidance to the task forces and to provide an opportunity through meetings at perhaps six-month intervals for staff of the divisions to express their views to departmental management. One group suggested that division chiefs might be selectively rotated as members of the support group so that they could get an overview of the concerns of staff in the department. Another suggestion was that the director might create an advisory group, perhaps composed of one staff member from each division, to permit a direct channel of communication from staff to departmental management. While there seems to be one view that perhaps the time has come to end the ADM Strengthening Exercise and to institutionalize the process through line management, other task force members appear to favor maintaining some channel of communication from the staff to the director's office.

10. While the task forces were not limited to the areas they could address, there were other areas that Mossop and I felt must be addressed if the change process was to be a success. It was for this purpose that we had prepared the action plan with which the exercise was launched and that included twenty-four areas in which there was to be some activity, in order to ensure that the change would be successful, and that we hoped would become a way of life within the department. . . . I am not satisfied that the level of change that I would like to have seen has yet occurred in the department, and I am convinced that considerable further effort is needed in order to make living with change the way of life in the department. Nevertheless,

on reading my report on progress on the original action plan, I am sure that you will recognize that probably at least 80 percent of the goals we had set have been achieved.

Discussion

11.   You will recall that when we introduced the program to strengthen ADM we defined its purpose as "the *initiation* of a process of improvement within ADM that ensures that services are delivered in an appropriate, efficient, and economic manner, and in an environment that supports job satisfaction and individual growth." There can be no doubt that this process has been initiated within the department. We should therefore consider that we have achieved our first objective and consider where we will go from here.

12.   I noted above when referring to the twenty-four points Mossop and I felt should be covered in order to ensure the change would be beneficial and continuing that I am not satisfied with the result, in spite of the fact that we have achieved 80 percent of our original objectives. The source of my dissatisfaction must lie somewhere within the 20 percent of the objectives not achieved.

13.   Looking back over the twenty-four actions, I find six in which I feel there is a significant gap between the expectation I had and the result. These are:

- the acceptance by departmental managers of the urgent need for change both in our approach to managing and in the nature of services provided
- the design of the career development system
- the systematic use of strategic planning, including the use of a strategic planning model
- a zero-based services review
- the development and implementation of departmental management information systems
- a department-wide training plan

14.   The reorganization of the ADM Director's Office has provided a personnel unit that is undertaking programs for the design

of the career development system and a department-wide training plan. The systems unit in the ADM Director's Office will be working during the next year on further development of the strategic planning model and refinement of departmental management information systems. The finance/controller unit in the ADM Director's Office will cooperate with the systems group on development of the management information systems and will also focus on a zero-based review of the services offered by the department. I am reasonably satisfied with the staff in place or about to assume responsibilities in these areas and with the fact that we will correct the above deficiencies within a reasonable period of time, provided we have the support of the line managers.

15.   I believe that the proviso just mentioned is, in fact, the principal factor in the failure of the ADM Strengthening Program to completely meet its objectives. The need for line managers to support the program was identified at the outset, and this is the reason it has been given first priority in the proposed action plan. Nevertheless, it was necessary to involve all the staff in the department in the exercise, and it was inevitable as a result that line managers would be a minority in any of the action groups. This risk was recognized and has become a fact, and the consequence now must be corrected.

Conclusion and Recommendations

16.   My principal conclusions on reviewing the strengthening plan as introduced to the department in October 1981 are:

- The program has met its objective in initiating a process of improvement within the department.
- The process for improvement must be continued if the department is to succeed in economically and efficiently providing the services the bank needs in a productive and fulfilling atmosphere.
- The restructuring of ADM Director's Office will make it possible to satisfactorily cope with the remaining deficiencies in the department provided that all supervisors and line managers support the effort.

- It is essential that I make it clear to the line managers what is expected of them and that these expectations be reflected in their performance plans with the clear understanding that if they are not met, then we will have to look for managers who will meet them.
- Some mechanism/procedure must be designed/communicated so that the bulk of the staff in ADM feel that they have the opportunity to communicate their concerns up the line.

17. Based on the above conclusions, I am implementing the following action plan to continue the strengthening of ADM:

- The ADM Director's Office has been restructured with four staff units focusing respectively on human resources, systems, financial management, and internal communications. Some of these staff units will be reinforced through recruitment of staff and consultants, which is already underway.
- I will be meeting with the two assistant directors and advisers from PMD on April 11 and 12, 1984, to reach agreement on managerial values to apply in ADM and on a program to communicate these values and to develop managers who will use them throughout the department.
- On April 18, 1984, the assistant directors and I will meet with assembled ADM staff managers to report on the ADM Strengthening Exercise and communicate the program to be followed in fiscal year 1985 to continue the strengthening process through a departmental management improvement program. We will also advise staff that they all have a responsibility to continue the spirit of the exercise but that henceforth their comments, suggestions, and issues should be communicated up the line until they obtain a satisfactory response.
- On April 19, 1984, the assistant directors and I will meet with the division chiefs to explain to them that the management improvement program will encompass the director, the assistant directors, and the division chiefs.

Performance plans for fiscal year 1985 will be based not only on work unit objectives for the year but also on an evaluation of each person's management practices (by self, supervisor, and subordinates). Support (training and counseling) to make identified needed improvements will be provided.

- Details will be discussed individually with each manager after the evaluations and in setting fiscal year 1985 objectives. This phase will be completed by June 30, 1984. More generalized training will be provided for lower-level managers/supervisors during fiscal year 1985 based on a general needs assessment.

18. I am convinced that through a program to follow up on the ADM Strengthening Exercise, using a top-down approach (starting with me) to improve managerial behavior and emphasizing the continuation of the many other activities initiated during the past two years, we will make significant improvement in ADM by the end of fiscal year 1985. Our fiscal year 1986 program will be based on an evaluation of where we stand one year from now.

19. In closing this last report, I must repeat my earlier expression of tribute to the dedication of the 170 staff (and process consultants), who have or are serving on task forces and subgroups. We have given them the opportunity to share in the managerial task of improving our business and changing the way we manage people in ADM. They have done this work while fully holding down the demands of their jobs. They have had to overcome apathy and opposition from others. Even though there is still work to be done, the department has come a long way as a result of their first-class effort.

William J. Cosgrove
Director, ADM

Demands on Change Planners in the Future

Looking back on the World Bank experience and other similar activities in which each of us has participated separately, we are convinced that change efforts are certain to be pro-active challenges in the years that lie ahead. We would, therefore, like to share with you some thoughts concerning the demands that will face change planners tomorrow.

Change within organizations will come about only if we define goals and objectives that are based on finite belief, concept, or theory. This generally is referred to as a parameter or cultural values approach. Many practitioners have tended to adopt a new method here, an unproved technique there, expecting some miracle, some peripatetic quick fix; but this manner of problem solving has had little effect on most organizations other than to disrupt their routine and separate them from the coin of the realm. Almost all organizations change over a lengthy period under the influence of many factors that can be nurtured and fed adroitly under a solid change process properly planned and appropriately fitted to the organization's present culture; seldom does this take place from hasty reorganization or introduction of a new fad sprung up in the garden of behavioral science.

Organizations will require new structures in order to cope with an overwhelming demand for flexibility. Traditional structures will not be adequate to deal with increasing complexity in size, finances, manpower, diversification, and interdependence. Among the more obvious and somewhat tried answers will be the task force, the project group, the matrix unit. The latter, particularly, permits an organization and its management to be pro-active rather than reactive, to adapt and respond appropriately, to use human resources to the best advantage. The matrix process, designed to help solve problems that cannot readily be reduced by conventional sub-systems, mental processes, or methods, is a special kind of problem-solving concept in both form and function. Drawing from the larger, formal, parent organization (and from outside sources as well, if need be), the men and women, the machines, and the procedures and techniques of diverse social and physical sciences, the matrix process integrates it all into a temporary force with the objective of doing what bureaucratic structure and routine method cannot handle. Upon completion of its task, the component parts of this force return to their former functional activities.

Change will come about within an organization only if there is encouragement and legitimization of constructive dissatisfaction. Too many managers feel compelled to put a lid on disagreement, stress, and conflict. Millions of creative ideas have been lost in climates that are incapable of allowing for honest differences in judgment and opinion. Pertinent points of view are often filtered out before they get to top management. The dictates of a pressing future are that a strictly win-lose concept will be a losing proposition, that win-win will be a winner. Openness, candor, and frankly faced feedback should not be equated with laxity or ineptness or considered to be hostility or obstructionism. To the contrary, confrontation and conflict are assets when used in a positive way; the real obstructionists are those managers whose fearfulness prompts them to shut off the ideas and contributions of their subordinates.

The successful change effort cries for an open system of communication. Although to possess information is to possess power, effective management does not monopolize information. The character and climate of an organization can be deduced from the way it extends or withholds information. As it is now and cannot be in the future, most people in most organizations do not feel that they have access to all the information they need to do their work well. Information is an outgrowth of communication, and it can be both stored and retrieved. The act of communication—which takes place only at the individual level—underlies all our attempts to work together and all we know about ourselves, about other people, about our environment. Each individual is concerned with what the other individual is trying to say and actually is saying— and with how the other individual hears and sees or interprets what he or she hears or sees. Even though the policies and standards of an organization, together with its cultural norms, enter into every communication process, we can consider in planning change only those interchanges between many individuals that form the fabric and networks of an organization system.

Development of the individual will become an important but collateral responsibility of future organizations. The obsolescence rate of people will make it necessary for individuals to cope with change in their own lives and careers, and to do this they will demand and receive organization interest and assistance. The continued growth of a service-oriented society will change the complexity and nature of many jobs and of many structures, and adequate use of members of minority groups will be a constant challenge in an evolving milieu. There will be pressure to evolve programs that use the total human resources of the country, with underutilized resources necessarily recognized at both the individual and organization levels. This means older workers, women, youths, the unskilled, blacks, and others will need support systems in order to develop and maintain their potential. Almost all workers, of whatever group or level of affluence, probably will plan and implement second, even third, careers within their lifespan. This is a fact of life that change planners will ignore at their own peril.

There is a need for practical and feasible centralization and decentralization of decision making throughout organizations. As was successfully demonstrated in the World Bank experience, the process of involving persons in decisions that they will help implement is an important aspect of productive management. Obviously, all such persons cannot and will not be involved in every decision, even though effective communication about decisions is an indirect level of involvement. The degree of participation will depend on the forces in the situation, in the leader, and in the subordinate groups. These forces also will provide guidelines for the degree to which an organization leader involves others in decision making that is relevant to their experience and competency. Some decisions should be decentralized down to specialized groups; other decisions should be centralized. Among the latter, of course, are those dealing with overall policy in finance, legal, and management information systems.

Change will occur most readily and effectively where team building is accepted as a management philosophy. Studies in psychology, sociology, and management clearly indicate that if an organization is to make maximum use of human resources and meet the highest level of each person's needs, it will function best in situations in which the individual relates successfully and smoothly to those natural groups of which he or she is a member and/or leader. Such well-knit and functioning face-to-face units will develop out of conditions that provide an interdependent relationship between a supervisor and those supervised. As organizations grow larger and more complex, the peer relationships of a work unit are even more crucial for purposes of accountability and productivity. A group usually can influence the larger system more easily than can an individual. Interunit collaboration will be essential; we can ill afford the luxury of vested interests and demolishing infighting.

A change effort is not going to be successful unless the organization is using properly individual contributions. Uncounted numbers of organizations are tying down and restricting people rather than providing quality control over contributions to what should be a common goal. The concept of sociotechnical systems is based on the reality that production and service alike require a work relationship structure and a technology that together relate human resources to technological resources. In this context, an organization's total system provides the set of human activities—together with interrelationships of these activities to the techno-physical-financial resources and processes—that make and deliver services and/or products. To think about an organization as a sociotechnical system helps make viable the man-machine conjunction of the future and assists in seeing it as an unending process of energy exchange. In the work place, in this electronic age, it will be essential to help people use all the technologies available while at the same time freeing them of unnecessary rules, regulations, and red tape.

Change efforts will be destined to fail unless there is equitable acceptance of the risks inherent in experimentation and innovation. Most people in many organizations have stopped taking risks, playing everything safe. Typical bureaucrats do not "stick their necks out," and survival dictates not taking chances. Where such a philosophy prevails, the organization is resting on dead center—functioning perhaps, but at a low level of efficiency. Change efforts in this kind of organization often resemble an attempt to lever a ton with a toothpick. A succeeding generation, in many cases, will have to cope with the same realities through experimentation simply because we do not know all the answers. We will need new forums, processes, and structures, as well as new approaches to human resources utilization and management.

Leadership in change efforts will require situational, rather than predetermined, choices and decisions. One of the great distortions of behavioral science research has been the belief that there can be one and only one correct management style. On the contrary, a manager sometimes needs to be directive, sometimes consultative, and even occasionally group oriented; it all depends on the people involved and the situation, and the existential situation demands diagnosis by the leader in achieving appropriate responses. A situational approach, reduced to its elementary truth, utterly depends on the situation existing from day to day, if not from moment to moment. A natural *leader,* and sometimes a *trained* manager, knows when and how to behave in accordance with the situation at hand. Beyond this, nevertheless, a question frequently asked by those who sense a need for and contemplate a change effort is: "How do I know whether change is needed or advisable?" A question also often posed by those about to enter or already engaged in a change effort is: "How do I know when my change effort is beginning to take hold successfully?" The answers to both of these queries are found in Table 9.

Table 9. Test for Change Effort Advisability and Success.

1. Organization is in touch with and responding to its external environment.
2. Subsystems are integrated toward a common goal.
3. Leadership is developing an employment commitment.
4. There are no isolated units.
5. Organization is willing to take planned and calculated risks.
6. There is appropriate emphasis on quality of work life.
7. Board policy is centralized; implementation and innovation are decentralized.
8. Organization quickly adapts and constructively changes.
9. Problems are solved at the lowest practicable level.
10. The system rewards creativity and innovative thinking.
11. Accountability is emphasized rather than control over people.
12. Organization instills high expectations.
13. Open communication is a way of life.
14. Conflict is managed productively and advantageously.

A major change effort seldom is initiated just for the hell of it. Nor is such an expenditure of resources often launched only on a suspicion that something might be correctable—*and,* if corrected, might produce more of something desirable, such as profit, efficiency, or peace. It takes really far-sighted leadership to recognize and go after the goals outlined in Table 9—and one of the reasons for our sharing our World Bank experience is that the World Bank had just such extraordinarily perceptive leadership. Far more typical, however, is the situation in which a perceived need for change is brought into sharp focus by an event, initiation, threat, or reality. An examination of the history of organization change efforts reveals these examples of unwelcomed initiators: the closing of two plants or the relocation of the principal headquarters; the threat of a takeover by another organization; a major decision about the product line, services made available, or purpose of the organization; foreign competition or a crucial union/management confrontation; the resignation, dismissal, or death of a chief executive officer—or the introduction of a new chief executive officer; strongly expressed dissatisfaction on the part of stockholders or serious questions raised by a board of directors; and, last, but ordinarily most critical, an acute and usually unexpected decrease in productivity, profit, self-respect, or public regard. These sometimes violent, nonacademic stimuli goad nonexceptional managers into actions that they hope will save an organization or better its performance. But, to be fair, it must be recognized that top managers are only human beings and that they have the same fear of the unknown that overtake all mere mortals. They know all too well that the best-planned change effort surely will—and usually should—affect their organization's style, culture, and leadership, that their own status is to be equally subject to review and revision, and that these realizations and the acceptance of change inevitably must lead down a road toward new and unfamiliar goals, policies, practices, and philosophies.

Toffler (1980, p. 10) capably elucidated a challenge to the leaders of our society when he wrote:

> Humanity faces a quantum leap forward. It faces the
> deepest social upheaval and creative restructuring of

all time. Without clearly recognizing it, we are engaged in building a remarkable new civilization from
the ground up. This is the meaning of the Third
Wave. Until now the human race has undergone
two great waves of change. . . . The First Wave of
change—the agricultural revolution—took thousands
of years to play itself out. The Second Wave—the rise
of industrial civilization—took a mere three hundred
years. Today history is even more accelerative, and it
is likely that the Third Wave will sweep across history
and complete itself in a few decades. We, who happen
to share the planet at this explosive moment, will
therefore feel the full impact of the Third Wave in our
own lifetime. The Third Wave brings with it a gen-
uinely new way of life based on diversified, renewable
energy sources, on methods of production that make
most factory assembly lines obsolete; on new non-
nuclear families; on a novel institution that might be
called the "electronic cottage," and on radically
changed schools and corporations of the future. . . .
The emergent civilization writes a new code of behavior for us, and carries us beyond standardization,
synchronization, and centralization, beyond the concentration of energy, money, and power. . . . Above all
. . . Third Wave civilization begins to heal the historic
breach between producer and customer, giving rise to
the "prosumer" economics of tomorrow. For this
reason, among many, it could—with some intelligent
help from us—turn out to be the first truly humane
civilization in recorded history.

Our eclectic approach to planned change in one department
at the World Bank apparently has been successfully responsive to
the thrown gauntlet that characterizes our civilization's Third
Wave—being on target, at least, in achieving wanted organization
goals, developing a systems perspective, and leading to improvement in the quality of work life for all the people who make up the
World Bank.

Reflective Comments

It may be superflous to add a final note about learnings in a chapter dealing with learnings. It is relevant, however, to observe how many learnings about change, both positive and negative, can be derived from an experience such as the one we enjoyed at the World Bank. Our concern is that the success achieved in one subsystem is deeply rooted in the cultures and norms of the total organization. While within the Administrative Services Department attitudes toward and acceptance of participative management did change, how will such change be sustained unless the whole culture of the World Bank moves in the same direction? Such a major shift will take time. It will require new policies, specially-designed executive training programs, and a supportive reward system. These advances are taking place, but in a large multinational institution a change toward participative management will not come all at once—because people experience readiness for change at differing paces.

References

Ackoff, R., Finnel, E. V., and Gharajedaghi, J. *A Guide to Controlling Your Corporate Future.* New York: Wiley, 1984.

Beckhard, R. "The Confrontation Meeting." *Harvard Business Review,* 1967, *45* (2), 66–72.

Beckhard, R., and Harris, R. *Organizational Transitions—Complex Change.* Reading, Mass.: Addison-Wesley, 1977.

Beer, M. *Organization Change and Development: A System View.* Santa Monica, Calif.: Goodyear, 1980.

Bennis, W. G. "A New Role for the Behavioral Sciences: Effecting Organization Change." *Administrative Science Quarterly,* 1963, *8,* 125–165.

Bidwell, R., and Lippitt, G. L. *Attitudes of Consultants and Clients to Research on the Consultation Process."* Unpublished paper, George Washington University, 1971.

Blake, R., and Mouton, J. *Corporate Excellence Through Grid Organization Development.* Houston, Tex.: Gulf, 1968.

Buber, M. D. *Dialogues on Realization.* (M. Friedman, Trans.) New York: McGraw-Hill, 1964.

Cameron, K., and Whetten, D. A. *Organizational Effectiveness: A Comparison of Multiple Models.* New York: Academic Press, 1983.

Carkhuff, R. R. *The Art of Helping Student Workbook.* Amherst, Mass.: Human Resource Development Press, 1980.

Chandler, D., Jr. *Strategy and Structure: Chapters of the American Industrial Enterprise.* Cambridge: Massachusetts Institute of Technology Press, 1962.

Crockett, W. J. "Introducing Change to a Government Agency." In P. H. Mirvis, and D. N. Berg (Eds.), *Failures in Organization Development and Change.* New York: Wiley, 1977.

Davis, K. "Evolving Models of Organizational Behavior." *Academy of Management Journal,* 1968, *8* (2), 27–38.

Deal, T. E., and Kennedy, A. A. *Corporate Cultures: The Rites and Rituals of Corporate Life.* Reading, Mass.: Addison-Wesley, 1982.

Egan, G. *The Skilled Helper: Models, Skills, and Methods for Effective Helping.* (2nd ed.) Monterey, Calif.: Brooks/Cole, 1982.

Farchex, C., Amado, G., and Laurent, A. "Organizational Development and Change." *Annual Review of Psychology,* 1982, pp. 343–370.

Foltz, J., Harvey, J., and McLaughlin, J. "Organization Development: A Line Management Function." In J. D. Adams (Ed.), *New Technologies in Organization Development.* (2nd ed.) La Jolla, Calif.: University Associates, 1975.

Gardner, J. "Toward a Self-Renewing Society." *Time,* 1969, *93,* 40.

Gazda, G. M. *Human Relations Development: A Manual For Educators.* Boston: Allyn and Bacon, 1973.

Georgiades, N., and Wilkinson, B. *Centre for Leadership and Organizational Resources.* Unpublished World Bank course materials. Bath, U. K., 1983.

Gulowsen, J. *Selvstyrte Arbeidsgrupper. På vei mot Industrielt*

Demokrati. [*Autonomous Work Groups Moving Toward Industrial Democracy.*] Oslo, Norway: Tanum, 1971.

Harrison, R. "Choosing the Depth of Organizational Intervention." *Journal of Applied Behavioral Science,* 1970, *6* (2), 118–201.

Herbst, P. G. *Socio-Technical Design: Strategies in Multidisciplinary Research.* London: Tavistock, 1974.

Hoff, B. *The Tao of Pooh.* New York: Penguin Books, 1983.

Huse, E. F. *Organization Development and Change.* (2nd ed.) New York: West, 1980.

James. U. S., and Oliver, L. W. *A Preliminary Assessment of the Impact of the Army's Organizational Effectiveness (OE) Program.* Alexandria, Va.: Army Research Institute for the Behavioral and Social Sciences, 1981.

Jayaram, G. "Open Systems Planning." In W. G. Bennis and others (Eds.), *The Planning of Change.* (3rd ed.) New York: Holt, Rinehart and Winston, 1976.

Langseth, P. *Selbstgesteuerte Arbeitsgruppen als Mittel zur Auslösung von Demokratisirung Prozessen in Einer Norwegian Bank.* [*How to Use Autonomous Work Groups in Order to Increase the Democracy in a Norwegian Bank.*] Dissertation 716, Handelschochschule, St. Gallen, Switzerland, 1979.

Langseth, P., and Werring, H. *Aktivt Personalarbeid.* [*Active Personnel-Work.*] (3rd ed.) Oslo, Norway: Tanum-Norlie Forlag, 1979.

Lewin, K. *Field Theory in Social Science.* New York: Harper & Row, 1951.

Lippitt, G. L. *A Handbook for Visual Problem Solving.* Bethesda, Md.: Development Publications, 1973.

Lippitt, G. L. *Organization Renewal.* (2nd ed.) Englewood Cliffs, N.J.: Prentice-Hall, 1982.

Lippitt, G. L. *A Look at the Future.* Springfield, Mass.: Springfield College Management Institute, 1983a.

Lippitt, G. L. *An Evaluation Report of the ADM Strengthening Project at the World Bank (Phase I).* Bethesda, Md.: Project Associates, 1983b.

Lippitt, G. L., and Swartz, D. "Evaluating the Consulting Process." *Journal of European Training,* 1975, *4* (5), 301–310.

McCaskey, M. B. *Framework for Analyzing Work Groups.* Case 9-480-009. Cambridge, Mass.: Harvard Business School Course Services, 1981.

Mager, R. F. *Preparing Instructional Objectives.* (2nd ed.) Belmont, Calif.: Fearon, 1973.

Margulies, N., and Wallace, J. *Organizational Change: Techniques and Applications.* Glenview, Ill.: Scott, Foresman, 1972.

Marrow, A. *Making Waves in Foggy Bottom.* Washington, D.C.: National Training Laboratory Institute, 1974.

Miles, R. M. "Organizational Effectiveness." In R. M. Miles (Ed.), *Macro-Organizational Behavior.* Santa Monica, Calif.: Goodyear, 1980.

Naisbitt, J. *Megatrends: Ten New Directions Transforming Our Lives.* New York: Warner Books, 1982.

Nicholas, J. M. "The Comparative Impact of Organization Development Interventions on Hard Criteria Measures." *Academy of Management Review,* 1982, 7, 531.

Niedzviecki, S. and Langseth, P. *Administrative Services Department Strengthening Handbook.* Washington, D.C.: World Bank, 1982.

Peters, T. J., and Waterman, R. W., Jr. *In Search of Excellence.* New York: Harper & Row, 1982.

Porras, J. I., and Berg, P. O. "The Impact of Organization Development." *Academy of Management Review,* 1978, 3, 249–266.

Rush, H. M. F. "Organization Development in Practice: A Comparison of O.D. and Non-O.D. Companies." *Organization Development: A Reconnaissance,* 1974, 605, 31–33.

Simon, H. A. *Models of Man.* New York: Wiley, 1967.

Steele, F. *The Role of the Internal Consultant.* Boston: CPI, 1982.

Steers, R. M. "Problems in the Measuring of Organization Effectiveness." *Administrative Quarterly,* 1975, 20, 128.

Stubbs, I. *Human Resource Audit.* Bethesda, Md.: Organization Renewal, 1982.

Thompson, J. D. *Organizations in Action.* New York: McGraw-Hill, 1967.

Thorsrud, E., and Emery, F. *Industrielt Demokrati, Representasjon pa styreplan i bedrifen.* [*Industrial Democracy, Employee Board Representation.*] Oslo, Norway: Universitetsforlaget, 1964.

Thorsrud, E., and Emery, F. *Mot en ny bedriftsorganisasjon.* [*Toward a New Organization.*] Oslo, Norway: Tanum, 1967.

Tichy, N. M. *Managing Strategic Change: Technical, Political and Cultural Dynamics.* New York: Wiley, 1983.

Toffler, A. *The Third Wave.* New York: William Morrow, 1980.

Vaill, P. "OD as a Scientific Revolution." Unpublished paper, George Washington University, 1973.

Vaill, P. "The Purposing of High-Performing Systems." *Organizational Dynamics*, Autumn 1982, *2* (2), 23–39.

Ware, J. *Managing a Task Force.* (Reference 9-478-022.) Boston: Intercollegiate Case Clearing House, 1981.

Waterman, R. W., Jr., and Peters, T. J. "Structure Is not Organization." *Business Horizons,* June 1980, *23*, 14.

Waterman, R. W., Peters, T. J., and Phillips, S. R. "Structure Is not Organization." *The McKinsey Quarterly,* 1982, *8*, 2–20.

Wedgwood, H. C. "Fewer Camels, More Horses: Where Committees Go Wrong." *Personnel,* July/August 1967, *44* (4), 62–67.

Weisbord, M. *Organizational Diagnosis: A Workbook of Theory and Practice.* Reading, Mass.: Addison-Wesley, 1978.

Index